BREAKING
through the
BARRIERS
LEADING MUSLIMS TO CHRIST

BREAKING
through the
BARRIERS
LEADING MUSLIMS TO CHRIST

ROSEMARY SOOKHDEO

Isaac Publishing
www.isaacpublishing.com

Breaking Through The Barriers

Published by Isaac Publishing, 6729 Curran Street, McLean VA 22101

Library of Congress Catalogue Number: 2010931076

ISBN 978-0-9825218-1-6

Printed in the United States of America

CONTENTS

PREFACE

This book is written in several sections, which together enable us to understand Muslims[1] better and how to reach them for Christ. To do this it is essential to know about the religion of Islam and be able to compare it to Christianity, at least at a basic level. Every chapter has been included to enhance this understanding. Part I deals with practical matters, and Part II with its Appendix outlines the main beliefs of Islam and how it differs from Christianity.

The first chapter in Part I is about how to get started. It provides clear cultural guidelines on our attitude and response to the various situations we are going to encounter in relating to Muslims. It also explains different types of relationship within the Muslim community and how it is appropriate for us to behave in these contexts.

Chapters two and three give an overview of Muslim culture from behind the scenes. They explain in detail the cultural norms we should expect to meet, including their differences from Western culture, and how we should interpret them.

Chapter four covers our proper response to Muslims within our own culture. This should enable us to avoid cultural blunders. It covers areas such as what we should do when we invite a Muslim friend for a meal, what type of gift we should bring on various occasions, what to do when a family member dies, and many more.

Chapter five explains how to share the Gospel effectively and lead a Muslim to the point of accepting Christ as Lord and Saviour.

Chapter one of Part II deals with what Muslims believe concerning prayer, fasting and giving. Again, it is only by knowing about these that we are able to present the living Christ to them.

Chapter two places Islam in the context of spiritual warfare. This is another aspect of Islam that is hidden behind the scenes. Folk Islam, which is an integral part of Islam, relates to subjects such as angels, demons, the evil eye and cursing. This is a very important topic, and we should understand something about it before we encounter Islam in any form.

Chapter three outlines some of the theological barriers that hinder Muslims from coming to Christ. Knowledge of these enables us to understand Islam in greater detail and can be very useful in evangelism. The chapter also highlights many of the differences between Islam and Christianity, including the one between *Isa* (the Jesus portrayed in the Qur'an) and the Jesus revealed in the New Testament. Understanding this is essential if we are to talk about Jesus to Muslims, as they will have a completely different view of Him. Other differences, such as Christians' assurance of heaven and knowledge of God (as distinct from knowledge that is just about God) can be very attractive to Muslims.

The appendix is a chart showing the differences between Islam and Christianity, as an essential guide for all Christians.

INTRODUCTION

A fter studying at theological college in London, I embarked with my husband Patrick on a ministry to the Muslim community throughout Britain. For a period of five years, in conjunction with the Evangelical Alliance, we conducted training seminars and mission outreaches throughout Britain on the theme "How to understand and reach Muslims".

Five years later, in 1975, we moved to the East End of London to establish a training and ministry centre to the Muslim community and to church plant amongst the local population. The area surrounding us was multicultural, with 40 different ethnic groups, and had a large Muslim population. We remained there for 23 years and in that time trained numerous groups, including missionaries and theological college students, in such subjects as "Ministry to Muslims" and "Urban Evangelism", as well as planting a number of churches.

To church plant in an area that at the time was the poorest and most violent in all of Britain was an uphill task. Even though our focus was on ministry to Muslims, we shared the Gospel with all those who came across our path. As a result the churches we planted were mainly multicultural ones.

Several times a year we brought together a team of young people recruited from universities and churches throughout Britain and the US to take part in mission outreach. They would be trained in "How to understand Muslim culture" and "How to get alongside Muslims". The team would be sent out in pairs to visit all the homes within approximately a mile radius (about 50,000) with the aim of sharing Christ.

One of my tasks was to lead and train the outreach team. When involved in church planting we could not expect people to come to us but went out to them and literally "sat where they sat". We tried in every possible way to identify with the local people and aimed to get inside their homes in order to share the Gospel or to invite them to a special event that we were holding. Amongst other activities we ran barbecues, showed films such as the Jesus film, opened a drop-in centre for people with problems and ran a special healing service on Sunday evenings once a month. We took people to hospital appointments, picked up children from school in emergencies and did everything possible to show Christ's love. We conducted Bible studies in homes with Muslim women. We held children's clubs during the school vacations and boys' and girls' clubs every week.

It was very interesting as we would never know what would happen each day and always had high expectations for what the Lord would do. Sometimes we would see people, including Muslims, so prepared by the Lord that they would come to Christ on the spot. This was divine appointment. Door-to-door visitation proved to be a great blessing and an encouragement to us. And from time to time we would visit a home where the person would tell us that all their life they had waited for this day.

We learnt through trial and error what would succeed and what would not. If something did not work we would try new strategies. We adapted our worship service to make it relevant to the needs of the local multi-cultural community. In our major church plant in Plaistow we had 28 nationalities fellowshipping in a thriving, vibrant church.

My experience of evangelism amoung Muslims in East London has been enhanced over the years by many interactions with Christians engaged in the same kind of ministry in other cultures and contexts. I have met and visited brave and effective evangelists in many different places and have learned much from them.

Over the centuries the Church has gone out of its way to avoid encounters with Islam. The Western missionary movement had fewer missionaries in the Muslim world than in any other part of the world, and has largely ignored the Muslims on our doorstep. With the contemporary refocus on Islam many people are beginning to have a burden for the Muslim world and also see the urgency of the task in front of us. However Muslim communities are becoming more conservative and are beginning to resist or actively stop any approach made to them by Christians. It is now the Muslims who are reaching out to us with their *dawa* (mission), and considerable numbers of Christians in nearly every country are converting to Islam every year. The Muslims have successfully copied many Christian mission strategies and methods and are using them to promote the expansion of Islam in the non-Muslim world.

PART I

1

HOW TO START SHARING
WITH MUSLIMS

I t had always been considered that it is difficult for Muslims to come to Christ. Yet today worldwide there are more Muslims becoming Christians than at any time in history. They are coming through national evangelists, friendships, the media, the internet, visions, dreams, healings and acts of God. As we encounter Muslims we have to trust and pray that we can be the means whereby they find Christ.

As Scripture commands us to love our neighbours, we need to show Muslims the love of Christ. They are human beings like us, and there must be no hatred or bitterness in our heart towards them. We do, however, need to draw a distinction between the people and their religion. We must love the Muslim, but as with all other religions we must be able to analyse and critique the religion itself. We must recognise that Islam is totally different from any other religion as it is more than just a religion — it is a religion, a culture, a legal system (*sharia*) and a political system all rolled into one. In fact, as it is a totalitarian system it could be classified as an ideology.

Many Christians in our day believe that all ways lead to God and that ultimately everyone will be saved and see heaven. They say that because God is love and acts in a loving manner to everyone it would be against His nature to send anyone to hell. If we believe this, there is no point in sharing our faith with the Muslim or with anyone at all. The difficulty with this position is that it is contrary to Scripture, such as John 3:16, the verse we know so well: "For God so loved the world that he gave his one and only Son, that whoever believes in him shall not perish but have eternal life."

And John 3:18 says: "Whoever believes in him is not condemned, but whoever does not believe stands condemned already because he has not believed in the name of God's one and only Son."

Where do we start?

We start just where we are in the situation we find ourselves. As Christians we need to believe that anyone who comes across our path in life has been sent from the Lord. Their coming is no accident of fate but according to God's plan and purpose. Therefore our Muslim contacts have been placed near us by God to enable them to hear the Gospel and be saved. The person might be a shopkeeper in whose shop we buy goods, or a fellow student in our college, a person who works with us or a parent that we meet in the school playground when picking up our children from school. It is the person we meet in the many arenas of everyday life.

> Anyone who comes across our path in life has been sent from the Lord.

What the Lord calls us to do is to grasp the opportunities that he gives us to share the Gospel. I was able to share Christ in a Starbucks in London only recently when I was drinking hot chocolate. I was sitting in a row of seats that looked out of the front window when I saw a bus go past with the slogan "There's probably no God". The person sitting beside me starting talking, and I was able to share that there is a God and we can know him through the Lord Jesus Christ. The person believed what was written on the bus. My final words were: "What happens if you are wrong and there is a God? Think of the implications." In sharing the Gospel with Muslims you actually start a step further along, as they already believe in the existence of God.

Muslims are openly sharing their faith today and are out for converts. They have no hesitancy in presenting Islam to students in universities and in the workplace. They now have their missionary societies in the West and most other countries, with missionaries who "live by faith" and go door to door. They have meetings in churches and schools presenting Islam in very attractive ways, and as a result numbers of evangelical Christians are becoming Muslims. We must remember that as we undertake ministry to Muslims today they will also try to persuade us and are out to make converts to Islam. They often reject any approaches by Christians while unashamedly promoting their own faith. We must be aware of this at the outset for the persuasion is very subtle and is meant to undermine our faith. They are well prepared, as they are given information from the mosque on what Muslims perceive to be the weak points of Christianity.

Barriers we need to overcome

The greatest barrier to overcome in sharing our faith with Muslims is that of fear. Fear of an unknown situation, a culture that seems so different from our own, people who look different, behave differently, speak in a different language and eat different food. It can be paralysing to contemplate what to say and how to say it. The thought goes through our mind: will we say the right thing or will we offend?

In some cultures this barrier is more difficult to surmount than in others. People in cultures that encourage reserve, politeness and inward hesitancy find it very hard. To be effective in sharing your faith with a Muslim all reserve must be set aside, as this could be misinterpreted as superiority or aloofness. We will need to be open and transparent in all speech and behaviour, to such an extent that when we are asked what can be perceived as an embarrassing question we can answer it openly and honestly. Any covering up or avoiding of a question will be seen as a lack of trust

A person who is single could be asked, "Why aren't you married?" as singleness is not the norm in Islamic culture. They will need to find an open and honest answer to this question. It is usually the older generation who ask it. A more difficult question is: "How much do you earn?" What the person is trying to establish is your social standing in society, which will help him or her understand you. These questions might go on a long time. We must remember that they are normal ones that many Asian Muslims would ask and are not considered rude or intrusive. Young Muslim people today in Western countries are less likely to ask them.

How do we start a conversation?

We can start a friendship with Muslims simply by conversations about ordinary, day-to-day activities. On every visit the conversation usually begins by asking about the welfare of family members, which may take some time. There could be a misunderstanding if you ask about the welfare of family members of the opposite sex by mentioning their names or their relationship to the person you are addressing. This has to be done in a more round-about way. For example, if a Muslim man has a wife who is ill, other men would ask, "How is the family?" or "How is the children's mother?"

The basic rule of Muslim culture that should never be broken

In Muslim culture, relationships between the sexes are totally different from those in Western and other cultures. Women in Islamic communities ideally speak only to women, apart from their male relatives, and the men in theory speak only to men, apart from the female members of their own household. A Muslim woman would have difficulty even speaking to, let

> In Islamic culture relationships across the sexes such as those in Western culture do not exist.

alone having a longer conversation with, a man who was not her husband.

In traditional Islamic societies all relationships are based either on the family or on same-sex relationships. This means that in Islamic culture casual relationships across the sexes such as those in Western culture do not exist.

The main reason why so many Christian women marry Muslim men and convert to Islam is that they break this norm of Muslim culture. Western women who marry

> A Christian woman who even tried to speak to a Muslim man would be completely misunderstood.

Muslim men find it impossible to have even a short conversation with a man outside the family. And if they do, they will most likely be accused of having an affair or affairs. This is often a very real and continual problem, and as such a conversation goes against the cultural norms it causes jealousy and suspicion within a marriage.

A Christian woman who even tried to speak to a Muslim man would be completely misunderstood, as he would think that she wanted to have a sexual relationship with him. If the man was married and his wife was present, she would think that the woman was trying to have an affair with her husband, and this would provoke feelings of jealousy and cause problems between husband and wife. Likewise if a Christian man was speaking to a Muslim woman the husband could suspect his wife was having an affair, and he might throw her out of the home, beat her or even in extreme cases kill her. If this might seem extreme, it is now well documented that having an affair or being perceived as having an affair is one of the main reasons why husbands kill their wives in so-called "honour killings". There are even extreme instances where a Muslim man has had a dream that his wife was having an affair and has ended up killing her.

Difficulties we encountered

At least twice a year in our ministry to Muslims in East London we would recruit a team of up to 30 young people from universities and churches to take part in a mission outreach into the local area. The plan was to go into the Muslim community and visit every home and shop to share the Gospel. The young people would first be trained for a couple of days on what to do and say and were then put in pairs for visitation. All the pairs were same-sex unless they were husband and wife.

If two girls were visiting homes they were told that if a Muslim man or a child came to the door of a home they should ask for the wife/mother. If she was at home the Muslim man would usually send his wife to the door. If she was not at home the girls were trained to say that they would come back another time. One important rule is that a Christian girl must never go inside the home if the wife is not present, and also she must not engage the man in conversation. The same applies to a man: if a Muslim woman came to the door, he was trained to ask for the husband and not to carry on any conversation with her. On nearly every mission we would have a problem, usually when a young lady encountering a young Muslim man at the door engaged him in conversation. In her eagerness to share Christ the conversation could last an hour or more. As a result a relationship was formed; the young man might come around to the church looking for the girl, and problems ensued. These general principles apply to all outreach and encounters with the Muslim community, and should never be broken.

Sharing with Muslim women

The Muslim woman's place is considered to be in the home, and her responsibility is doing the housework, cooking and looking after the children. Whereas the majority stay at home some do go to work to increase the income of the family. There are now many young Muslim women who are well-educated and have careers. But even if a wife works, the husband will never help with the housework or cooking as these are considered to be women's work. Men, however, do the cooking on very special occasions such as weddings.

In outreach to Muslim women, the best time to visit the home is always in the early afternoon after she has finished her housework and before she picks up the children from school. The husband is usually at work during this time and she can be very lonely. If the husband is at home and he tries to engage in conversation, it is best to answer as briefly as possible and then proceed with the conversation with his wife. If the husband or any other man is present, seriousness is appropriate, as smiling and laughing can be misunderstood, and over-familiarity can be interpreted as a sign of a bad character. Even just looking at someone of the opposite sex can cause problems, and prolonged eye contact must be avoided. If men are present and you want to communicate something to them you will need to address the conversation to the wife. I really need to emphasise that this principle does apply in the West just as much as in any situation overseas.

If the wife goes to the kitchen it is wise to go with her to avoid being left alone with her husband, who will try to engage you in conversation. It is perfectly acceptable to do this. Remember that some of the best spiritual conversations and friendships are forged in the intimacy of the kitchen.

What do we talk about?

As we befriend Muslims we begin to realise that we have more in common with them than we thought in regard to basic human issues and life. For example, Muslims are interested, as we are, in the education and the bringing up of their children, and are very keen to talk about these subjects. Food and cooking are important for the women, and they will be very pleased to explain anything in regard to this. Muslims enjoy talking and explaining about their country of origin, which is always extremely interesting. In fact I have found that the conversations I have in Muslim homes are very similar to those in any home. If we live in the same country we are affected by the same issues.

> It is important to be a good listener and not to dominate the conversation.

It is important to be a good listener and not to dominate the conversation to such an extent that it becomes difficult for anyone to get a word in edgeways. However a balance needs to be kept and long silences avoided at all costs. We will also need to show a genuine interest and concern for the person – in other words, the love of Christ for the person.

Sorting out marital difficulties in a Muslim home

If a member of a Muslim family confides a family problem there is very little that you are able to do about it, except to be a listening ear. This is what the person would expect. They would not expect you to try and sort out the problem. Why is this?

You are never able to sort out family problems within a Muslim home, as the Muslim community has a family mechanism that is always used to sort out marital and family difficulties. A Muslim woman sorts out serious difficulties with the husband by returning to her family home and then dictating terms to her husband from a distance. The family then enters a period of negotiation until a compromise is reached. Of course this system falls down when her family are in a different country. It is then that she can feel isolated and vulnerable.

I remember the time when I tried to help a Muslim wife sort out her problems. Late one night she arrived at our door, as she had run away from her husband to solve her problems while living with us. She stayed with us for a couple of days and we were unfortunately caught in the middle. It got rather messy and difficult and it certainly was a lesson for the future never to be forgotten. The husband was very angry that his wife had gone outside the family, as that had shamed him.

How to be effective in reaching Muslims for Christ

In our years of Muslim evangelism we found that Muslims had varying degrees of commitment to Islam. There were some very strict and hard-line Muslims who were completely opposed to Christianity and were interested only in arguing against Christianity and promoting Islam. Their hearts were hardened to the Spirit of God. There were those whose hearts were more open and who were genuinely interested in having conversations about Christianity, and those who were spiritually seeking and had really open hearts. In our evangelism we had to manage our time for the most effective results, as we could have spent all of our time with the people whose hearts were hardened or those not really interested in spiritual issues. We prayed that the Lord would give us the discernment to know whose hearts were open to the Spirit of God and we concentrated on those. However, if you have next door neighbours who are Muslim, whatever their heart is like, it is important to reach them with the Gospel, as the Lord has placed them across your path. But if you know many Muslims you need to pray strategically that the Lord will guide you to the right ones on whom to spend time and prayer.

There was a missionary to Muslims who lived near us in East London who spent ten years in the area. Just before he left he came to visit us and said that one Muslim family whom he had visited for many years had finally invited him to a meal. He considered it a breakthrough. In ministry to Muslims it would be normal to be invited to a meal at an early stage. If it takes years to be invited any time spent with that person could be considered a waste.

It is easy to have only a social relationship

You have to decide at the beginning of ministry to Muslims that you mean business with God with regard to sharing the Gospel. It is very easy to have a friendship with a Muslim while providing no spiritual input. We thus forgo our Christian responsibility. Once a friendship develops it becomes more and more difficult to share Christ if we have not done so from the beginning. You may say, "My life speaks of my faith," but that is not sufficient; there also has to be verbal input. Sharing of our faith should come naturally, always undergirded with prayer. It is important to show that our faith is very important to us, but of course it is the Lord who saves His people.

The Muslim way of maintaining a good relationship

Muslims from an Asian culture believe that a good relationship with a person must be maintained at almost any cost. To keep the relationship they will tell you what they think you want to hear, rather than the facts as they are. This means there is a very grey area between yes and no. No is not as definitive as we might expect it to be. Yes can mean no and no can mean yes. We found this very difficult when we invited our Muslim friends to some special event. They would assure us that they were very keen to come but were only saying that to please us and maintain good relations.

> Muslims from an Asian culture believe that a good relationship with a person must be maintained at almost any cost.

The Muslim is very careful not to "lose face" or to be belittled in front of others. For example, if a man loses an argument or is ignored in front of others he will "lose face" and be shamed. This is a very important part of Muslim culture. It is said that it is often better to lose an argument than lose a friend.

With Muslims it is normal to speak about spiritual issues

In the West we are often hesitant to share our faith openly with anyone, as faith can be a very private affair. It is said in Britain that the two subjects you do not discuss in public are religion and politics. Also an old evangelistic strategy says that you must earn your right to speak about your faith to Muslims, so only after establishing a relationship or friendship with a Muslim can you, in time, speak about your faith.

> Muslims will speak readily about their faith and expect us to do the same.

However, in Islamic culture it is quite normal to speak about spiritual issues in everyday conversation, and in fact it would be abnormal not to do so. Everyday life and religion are so intertwined for the Muslim that a separation is not possible. Thus Muslims will speak readily about their faith and expect us to do the same. As Christians we should not be shy or diffident about speaking of our faith with Muslims, but readily share what we believe, though with wisdom and sensitivity. I would expect on every visit to a Muslim home or any conversation with a Muslim to offer some form of spiritual input. That would be normal and expected of me. Many people are unaware of this and it can be one reason for failure in ministry to Muslims.

There was one occasion, which I shall never forget, when I more than met my match. I visited a Muslim woman in hospital, who taught children Arabic at the local mosque. For every testimony of mine, every answer to prayer, she had one equally miraculous. I have often reflected on this woman and wondered whether what she was saying was actually rooted in reality or was just to match what I was saying. I shall never know, but maybe what I said that day might have been more effective than I realised. I trusted that the word of God would not return void.

Is debate effective?

Very few Muslims come to Christ through debate. The topics are usually selected by them and are meant to put Christians on the defensive. These include "Is the Bible the word of God?" and "Is Jesus the Son of God?" Topics such as "What are the nature and characteristics of a true prophet?" or "Can we be sure that when we die we will go to heaven?" are more suitable. Much effort is put into debate with very little result. We need to get Muslims onto our ground and our agenda, rather than always being on theirs.

2

HOW TO UNDERSTAND MY MUSLIM NEIGHBOUR

When getting alongside our Muslim neighbours, the first thing we need to realise is that our cultures are very different, and we need to understand their culture in relation to our own. We need to be able to speak, share and behave in a way that is not offensive to them and makes our Christian witness and testimony more effective.

In the West many Muslim families can appear to be very Western

Appearances can be very deceptive, as many Muslim families appear very Western to the outsider but behind the scenes conform to Muslim patterns of behaviour and culture. It is only as we get behind the scenes in a Muslim home that we realise how radically different are the culture and the way of life. One major difference is that Islam provides a structure for every part of life, from the way you enter a house, to where you sit in a room, how to pray, how to dress, how to fast – to name just a few examples. Muslims are required to enter a house with their right foot and always to eat with their right hand. Everything is clearly laid out with rules and regulations, leaving little room for self-expression or freedom as we know it.

When a Muslim community is very small, Muslims may take on the prevailing culture of the country to some degree, and the individual becomes more important. As the Muslim population increases in size it solidifies into communities and usually resumes all the aspects of Islamic culture. Religion here is a communal matter, the community being more important than the individual. This point can be difficult to understand as for most Western Christians religion is an individual and private matter. Not so with Islam.

The differences between Christian culture and Islamic culture

In the West living our life is of primary importance, whereas in the Islamic world religion is of primary importance. In the West we can find it is very difficult to understand a society where religion is the most important premise of a whole community, where religion is more important than life. However, among Christians in non-Western countries the Christian faith has more importance in relation to day to day living and is often the pivotal point of people's lives. We can see a total dedication and commitment to Christ in every realm of their life that can often be missing in the West.

Muslims are under the misconception that all Western countries are Christian countries and that everyone who lives in them are Christians. We do need to point out this misconception at some point and show them the true nature of a Christian. This can be a marvellous opportunity for sharing our faith and what it means to us.

Understanding Muslim loyalties

Muslims believe that the non-Muslim world, especially what they perceive to be the Judeo-Christian world, is against them and hates them. They can also have a deep-rooted hatred for the West, especially for the US and Israel. For example, they believe that a Jewish conspiracy is directed against them and that the West is at war with Islam and wants to destroy it. In Western countries Muslims see themselves as a persecuted minority that is poor, marginalised and despised. As Christians we need to show them the love of Christ, and that we have no hatred in our heart for them.

The Muslim world is set apart by the strength of their community, and the community takes priority over the individual. The individual's will and desires must always be subject to this community, and the community is in turn subject to the *umma*, or the world-wide Muslim state. This *umma* transcends race, nationality and culture. The primary loyalty of Muslims is to this global Muslim state and overrides any loyalty to the nation-state. This can produce divided loyalties in times of war or conflict. Although Muslims are divided amongst themselves, many close ranks in the face of an outside threat or what they perceive to be a threat. This happened when a Danish cartoonist portrayed Muhammad in a way that Muslims considered to be blasphemous. Many in the Muslim community worldwide were outraged and showed their anger in violent ways. Muslims also have an unwavering loyalty to each other when promoting the cause of Islam.

> As Christians we need to show them the love of Christ, and that we have no hatred in our heart for them.

For most Western Christians religion has become a private matter and is not subject to community pressure. There is no longer a concept of a worldwide Christendom comparable to the Muslim *umma*. However, Christians are united in the Biblical concept of the fellowship of all believers; that is, we are one with our brothers and sisters in Christ throughout the world.

Muslim society is based on the principle of "honour" and "shame"

Western culture and Islamic culture are based on completely different worldviews that are diametrically opposed in various ways. In the West we still have the remnants of a Judeo-Christian ethic, which makes clear distinctions between right and wrong. Although strict Muslims do have a concept of right and wrong, based on sharia rules regarding what is forbidden and what is allowed, Muslim society as a whole is not undergirded with this ethic and does not have these clear distinctions. The basis of Muslim society is that of honour and shame.

> **Western culture and Islamic culture are based on completely different worldviews that are diametrically opposed in various ways.**

It can be very difficult for us to understand a society that does not share our concept of right and wrong but instead is founded on a completely different worldview. This is particularly hard for us as Christians, as we are taught what is right and wrong as a fundamental part of Christian doctrine. We believe that what is wrong is sin before God, and we are commanded to be holy as Christ is holy. For Muslims it is their religion that dictates what is acceptable and unacceptable; the idea of right and wrong rarely becomes a factor.

One of the most important concepts in Islamic culture is that of family honour or *izzat*. This is maintained by conforming to the norms of the society and by the absence of any visible shame. Conformity is valued, as it brings honour and social prestige to the family. Honour is achieved by, for example, marriage, the passing of exams and giving birth to a boy. You can never confer honour on yourself, it comes from others by what they see or think they see. Honour is given to a family, a tribe or even a nation. A whole nation can be honoured or shamed and "lose face" in the sight of the world.

Individualism as we have it in the West is criticised by Muslims, as they believe that it does not benefit the family, and lack of conformity can lead to shame from the community. To maintain conformity, children are readily told if their behaviour is shameful, which enables them to learn the boundaries of personal behaviour.

The causes of shame

Shame can be caused by, amongst other things, not looking after your family, by losing your temper and shouting insults at a person, by harmful gossip and even by failure. In cases of failure, unless blame can be passed to another person, suicide can be seen as an honourable way out.

If a member of the family is responsible for any wrongdoing, or if they are in circumstances that could be conceived as shameful, this has at all costs to be kept within the family circle and hidden from the outside world; otherwise the family will be shamed. Even the birth of a baby girl can be considered shameful. Therefore honour and shame become the controlling force in people's lives.

Shame is not only an act against accepted norms or values, but it can also include the discovery by outsiders that the act has been committed. A person who has done a shameful act must conceal it, for revealing the disgrace is to commit another disgraceful act. To avoid shame, lying or concealment is seen as honourable and therefore the right thing to do. However, if a shameful act cannot be covered up it must be avenged.

Here we enter the realm of honour killings. For example, if a Muslim girl was engaged and then decided to break off the engagement, the family would feel that she had brought shame on them. In these circumstances many Western parents might be thankful that their daughter had not married the wrong man and ended up in an unhappy marriage. But in Muslim culture, the fact that the girl felt that she could not go through with the marriage for whatever reason would not be acceptable, and the likelihood that the marriage would have been unhappy is irrelevant. Likewise if a wife has an affair, or is even perceived by the husband or his relatives to be having an affair, she brings shame on the family. Shame is paramount.

In Muslim societies the fear of bringing shame is used as the controlling force in people's lives, and as a result people do not have the freedom to act as they want. They must always act honourably, to uphold the honour of the family at all times. This may mean, for example, that a married woman is not free to go out alone, work or

In Muslim societies the fear of bringing shame is used as the controlling force in people's lives.

talk to men other than family, as people will think she is flirting or having an affair and this will cause shame.

One family told me that if their daughter was beaten by her husband they would do nothing about it, as to take action would bring shame on the entire family. They would rather keep their honour and let their daughter suffer. As long as the violence was hidden from the outside world they would be satisfied.

The apportioning of honour and shame

Whilst in theory codes of honour and shame refer to the behaviour of both men and women, in practice honour is seen as men's responsibility and shame is usually apportioned to the woman. Inherent in this division is the concept of female sexuality, which Muslims believe needs to be controlled. We see this with the restrictions placed upon women and especially young girls. Women can be confined to the home, not permitted to go to work and forced to wear the *burqa*. It is because of these cultural norms that Islam traditionally has separate places for men and women where women speak only to women (apart from male relatives) and men ideally speak only to men (apart from female relatives).

Honour killings

For Muslim women virginity before marriage and fidelity afterwards are considered obligatory, and men are expected to control their female relatives. If a woman strays, it is widely believed that the dignity of the man can be restored only by killing her. As a result the slightest sniff of scandal can be a death warrant. Honour killings can be carried out on the flimsiest of grounds, such as a man claiming that he dreamt his wife had betrayed him. Communities are almost always supportive of these murders.

Every year worldwide there are hundreds of honour killings. Currently there are about twenty honour killings a year in Britain, and there are fears that the numbers will increase. The Metropolitan Police Service has formed a task force to increase its understanding of honour killings and to help it to investigate the murders and better help those who may be at risk.[1]

Honour killings are male, gender-based violence, which can be perpetrated by cousins, fathers, brothers, uncles, sons or any other male relative against a woman. A son can kill his mother if he believes she is having an affair, though there might be no proof of it. A father can kill his daughter. The reason is simply that they believe the woman has stepped out of line by her behaviour, perhaps by refusing an arranged marriage, or by what she wears, or by sexual misconduct. They believe she must be punished to restore the family honour.

The Yones family

The Yones family arrived in Britain in 1993 from northern Iraq. Once in Britain their daughter Heshu mixed with friends from all cultures. Her father grew increasingly distressed that she was not living according to Muslim values and tried to beat her into submission. But she continued to wear pretty dresses and enjoy a social life and attempted to placate him by dressing down at home and putting on make-up only when she was away from the family. She was terrified that her father would discover that she had a boyfriend.

Her letters, found after she was killed, showed that she was planning to run away from home and to start a new life. In one of the letters she told her father that she wanted to be alone and that he should not try to track her down. When an anonymous letter arrived revealing that his daughter had slept with her boyfriend, his worst fears were confirmed. In a rage he confronted his daughter, slit her throat and repeatedly stabbed her. He was horrified at what he believed was a stain on the family's name and was desperate to restore his honour, which he believed could be done only by killing her.

> **Most honour killings are characterised by extreme secrecy.**

Many such men have no fear of the law and are convinced such killings are an acceptable way to avenge damage to family honour. They may collude with other family members to kill their relatives. These crimes are an ever-increasing phenomenon in multicultural Britain and such is the protective nature of the families and communities in which they occur that outsiders rarely become aware of the victim's sufferings. If they do intervene it is usually too late, as most honour killings are characterised by extreme secrecy.[2]

Apologising is seen as weakness

There is no concept of guilt and forgiveness in Islam as we understand it in Christianity. This has repercussions in attitudes and culture, as Muslims can appear very self-righteous. For example, it is very difficult for Muslims to apologise, as apology implies weakness, and any sign of weakness brings shame. We see from recent surveys that some Muslims still have difficulty in accepting that 9/11 was perpetrated by Muslims, and constantly blame all and sundry. Because of this they are constantly persuaded by conspiracy theories readily to pass blame on to others. They can be considered to have developed a victim mentality in which they see themselves and the religion of Islam as under constant attack.

MUSLIM CULTURE AND THE FAMILY

How to greet a Muslim

The Muslims' greeting amongst themselves is *Salam Alekum*, which means, "Peace be with you." They then reply, *Wa-alekum as-salam*, meaning, "And unto you be peace". Many Christians give this greeting to Muslims unaware that many Muslims in their hearts do not receive it.

In Muslim culture men greet men and women greet women. Women usually greet one another with a kiss. Men may greet women but it will usually be with a nod and at a distance, as in many Muslim societies women never shake hands with men. However, in the West a woman may shake a man's hand if he offers his hand first; she is then obliged to take it. It is wise for her not to offer her hand first.

When you enter a room on Muslim visitation, you will need to acknowledge those present, whether by handshake, kiss or nod. It is good to be aware that prolonged or even eye contact between the sexes must be avoided, as it can send the wrong message. Eye contact in Muslim culture has sexual connotations and implies that you have a sexual interest in the person.

Prestige and the Muslim family

In Muslim culture age brings respect, and the older a person the more respect is given to them. This is a reversal of Western culture where elderly people are often marginalised and many are given little respect. The eldest male member has the place of honour as the head of the family, and will be responsible for all decision-making, such as buying a home or arranging a marriage.

When a son marries it brings prestige to the family, and in most instances the son will bring the bride into the family home, and they will live as an extended family. The daughter-in-law will then be expected to clean and cook under the watchful eye and direction of her mother-in-law. What may be surprising to us is that the most important woman in the home is the mother of the husband, and this is generally where the husband's loyalties lie, not with his wife. If the mother has died the most important woman is then the first wife of the eldest son.

When a woman gives birth to a son she gains prestige and status within the community, and will be known as the mother of Ahmad or whatever name the son is given. If she has a daughter first rather than a son shame will be brought on the family, and the birth can go unannounced. The husband can be angry if the wife gives birth to several girls, and he can be offered condolences as in a funeral.

> When a woman gives birth to a son she gains prestige and status within the community.

This has an effect on the mother, and she may be distressed at the birth of a girl and also feel ashamed, as she knows that what is really desired is a son. Muslims still believe that the sex of the child is determined by the mother even though medical evidence proves the opposite. If you are visiting a Muslim home where a girl has just been born, wisdom is needed not to offer congratulations readily when the husband or other family members are present.

Girls are certainly not valued the same as boys, as it is considered that their purpose in life is just to marry and then leave the family home to live with their in-laws. A son is an investment for the future, whereas a daughter is an investment for another family.

There is also the issue of the dowry that has to be given when a girl marries, making her a very expensive drain on the family finances.

Muslim names

In Biblical times the choice of a name was very important as it denoted character, and names were chosen with great care. In the West we often have first names that are used through the generations. We may give a child the name of an aunt or someone who is special to us and whom we want to remember. Muslims never choose the name of a living relative, but rather select a name because of its meaning. For example it is very common for a Muslim boy to be called Muhammad or after one of the prophets.

Muslim men and women may change their names several times during their lifetime. For example a woman may be given a name at birth, and a new one at adolescence, and then have her name changed on marriage. It may also be changed after the birth of her first-born son. Common names for women are ones from the Qur'an such as Mary or Miriam, or Aisha, who was Muhammad's favourite wife. A Muslim woman may keep her father's name after marriage, or take her husband's first name as her surname rather than taking her husband's name. This can be very confusing to us as it means that she will have a different surname from her husband and children. Another complication is that some children are given their surname as their first name. This means that in a family, the husband, wife and children can all have different surnames. Whereas this is quite difficult in Western countries the practice seems still to be followed.

A name change can also take place when a person's circumstances change or after recovering from an illness. If they believe an evil spirit has caused the illness, they might change their name to protect themselves from a reoccurrence so that the evil spirit cannot recognise them.

The role of young Muslim girls

It is usual for Muslim girls to leave school as soon as possible and then stay at home to do the family cooking and cleaning until they marry. Some do go on to take training courses, but further education is not generally seen as essential for girls, as the Muslim family's priority is to educate the males in the family.

Muslim girls who do manage to go to university see it as the only time in their life when they can have freedom to do as they please. They may travel to university in a *hijab* or conservative Muslim dress and remove it as soon as they get there. It is quite usual for them to adopt some form of western dress rather than traditional clothing. Many are leading a double life.

After leaving school a young girl will not be allowed to have any contact with the opposite sex, as there is no concept of dating in Islamic culture. The parents see this as being for the girl's own good: she will be protected; no harm will come to her; and she will be pure and a virgin when she gets married. The ultimate shame is producing a child outside of marriage. The excessive zeal with which girls must be guarded and their virginity protected makes them an almost intolerable burden on the family. Therefore husbands will be found for them and they will be handed over to their in-laws as soon as possible. After marriage a girl belongs to the husband's family.

> There is also no concept of courtship in Muslim culture.

Engagement and marriage in Islam

There is no concept of singleness in Muslim culture, and a question mark can hang over women who remain single. It is considered that all women need male relatives to protect them.

There is also no concept of courtship in Muslim culture, and couples might or might not meet before marriage. The norm is an arranged marriage, and that is usually with someone from a person's country of origin. The majority of arranged marriages are with first or second cousins, and a marriage can be seen as a means of getting family members to the West. In the UK, because of the frequency of marriage among first cousins, there are high rates of genetic abnormalities within the Muslim community[1]. If a marriage is arranged outside of the family, money and social standing play an important part in the marriage contract. There is no notion of falling in love in Muslim culture as we know it in the West, and this would not be considered of any importance.

Engagement as a prelude to marriage is much more important in Muslim culture than in the West, and to break this off brings shame on the family. Very few young people would have the courage to do this; most would just go through with the marriage. On her wedding day a girl cannot appear happy, as she is leaving her family, and out of respect for them she must appear sad. Her husband's family will now be more important to her than her own family.

Some young girls from age eleven to thirteen are taken back to their country of origin and are married to a relative, and then a few years later

> **A Muslim man can marry a non-Muslim woman and would expect her to convert to Islam on marriage.**

they return to the West with their husband. There are many cases of forced marriage where the girl or even the boy are tricked or forced into returning to their country of origin, by being told that a close relative is sick or that they are going for a vacation. All this causes stress and hardship for many young Muslims who want a western-style marriage with love as a factor. However, very few have the courage to stand against their parents and choose their own marriage partner, even though many would like to do so. To choose your own marriage partner would generally mean being disowned by the family, and the price for many is too high to pay.

A Muslim man can marry a non-Muslim woman and would expect her to convert to Islam on marriage and bring up the children as Muslims. Muslim women however are allowed by sharia to marry only Muslim men. Even if a man agrees to convert to Islam before or on marriage, it is still very difficult, sometimes impossible, for a Muslim woman to marry him.

Muslim women and friendship

Muslim women look to other women for companionship and relationships rather than to their husband. A friendship with a Muslim woman is very important for her and cannot be taken lightly or considered to be casual, as friendships for her are considered to be for life. This is something we need to remember in our Muslim visitation.

Divorce and the Muslim woman

Divorce can take place very easily in Islam and the power of divorce resides in the hands of the man. It is not considered shameful for a man to divorce his wife for whatever reason, though it is considered very shameful for a woman to initiate a divorce, and this will affect the whole extended family. In Islamic countries where there is sharia law, for the man to say, "I divorce you," three times constitutes a divorce. However, there are some countries, such as Tunisia and Egypt, where a woman can initiate a divorce.

In many Muslim countries, when a man divorces his wife she may lose everything (depending on the marriage contract) but keeps the dowry. If a Muslim woman becomes a widow or marries again, the children stay with the father or the father's family, as they are considered to be his property. In many Muslim countries it is virtually impossible for women to divorce. If they do manage to divorce they would usually end up leaving the marriage empty-handed. In Western countries, of course, this does not apply if the couple are legally married according to the laws of the country.

However, in Britain many Muslim women are finding that they are not legally married according to British civil law and are leaving the marriage with the much lesser rights of a cohabitee. When they were married at a mosque ceremony with no accompanying civil ceremony they assumed, wrongly, that the marriage was a legal one in the eyes of British law. (But only 160 mosques out of about 1,700 are registered for legal marriage in Britain, and without an accompanying civil ceremony the marriage is not a legal one.[2]) These marriages are in fact sharia marriages. This means that if the relationship breaks down, only sharia law is implemented, and there is no legal divorce procedure. The man has only to say, "I divorce you," three times and the couple are legally divorced according to sharia law. Sharia law is to the woman's detriment in cases of divorce and also those of bereavement, as she will not be legally entitled to a spouse's share of the assets as under British law. This will be the fate of all Muslim women in Western countries as sharia family law is introduced into their community. In the West, as women become aware of their rights, many are divorcing their husbands if they have a legal marriage according to British law.

It is a very common custom in Muslim societies for the man to threaten divorce without really intending to go through with it. This is a means of controlling his wife to make sure that she is obedient to him.

Polygamy permitted in Islam

It says in the Qur'an that a man can have up to four wives at one time (4:3): "...marry of the women who seem good to you, two or three or four..."

Many people ask if this really happens in the West. Do Muslim men here take more than one wife? The answer is yes: Muslim men do have more than one wife in western countries. But how can this happen and not be called polygamy, which is against the law of the country? The second and third marriages that take place in the

UK are sharia marriages with no civil ceremony accompanying the ceremony at the mosque. They are in fact not legal marriages in the UK and as a result not legally polygamous.

There can also be a second or third wife in the husband's country of origin whom the husband marries after arriving in the UK and may visit for periods of time. As long as these wives do not enter the UK this is not seen as polygamy. This is now becoming a major issue in western countries. However, if a man had a polygamous marriage before he entered the UK the women are all recognised as his wives. In this sense, polygamy is recognised in UK law.

Polygamy is supposed to occur only with the consent of the other wife or wives, but in reality this is rarely required. Polygamy causes great pain, suffering and dissension within a family and leaves women in a very weak position. It can also have damaging consequences in the up-bringing of the children.

The discipline of women

Qur'an 4:34 says, "So good women are the obedient, guarding in secret that which Allah hath guarded. As for those whom you fear rebellion, admonish them, and banish them to beds apart and scourge them. Then if they obey you, seek not a way against them."[3]

This verse actually permits a man to discipline his wife. The man has a responsibility to admonish his wife, the right to desert her sexually by moving into a separate bed, and the right to beat her to correct any rebelliousness in her behaviour. The word "rebellion" refers to any disobedience on the part of the woman, not simply a refusal to engage in sex.

> Polygamy causes great pain, suffering and dissension within a family

Islam and modernity

Islam is a culture that thinks and behaves in different ways from those of Western culture. The question is to what degree Islam can embrace modernity. The more radically Islamic a society becomes, the more there tends to be a deterioration in the position of women, and the more their rights are denied. The more liberal a Muslim society becomes the more rights women have.

There is now much more discussion among Muslims on women's rights in Islam, especially in the West, but also in some Muslim countries. Some Muslim women's Human Rights groups, such as the "Sisters of Islam" in Malaysia, have been speaking up on these issues. But so far little progress has been made in addressing the inequality of women, because this is rooted in Islamic sharia concepts.

The problem facing the Muslim community today is how to be both modern and Muslim. The difficulty is that many Muslims perceive modernity as synonymous with secularism, which is seen in a very negative light. They

> The more radically Islamic a society becomes, the more there tends to be a deterioration in the position of women.

look at the postmodern secular society of the West and do not want to be identified with it. They see the breakdown of the family and society and consider society to be morally corrupt. Some say that it is impossible and undesirable for Islam to embrace modernity.

4

POINTERS IN YOUR EVANGELISM TO MUSLIMS

I n the West good timekeeping is an essential part of our culture, but this is not the case in Islamic culture, as Muslims have an entirely different concept of time. People to them are more important than time, and as a result they are not ruled by or dependent on the time factor. Relationships are of primary importance. This means that it is not possible to go into a Muslim home for just ten minutes, as we would in many western countries. I would allow the minimum of one hour for a visit, and the question is whether one hour is enough. One basic rule of reaching Muslims is that you have to give time to it.

Dress is important

In Muslim communities the women will be well covered, with clothes that are loose and not transparent. Their dress will be modest and will cover from the front of the neck to the wrist and as far as the ankle and will not show the outline of the body. Wearing clothing that is too tight is considered immoral and brings shame on the family. The woman's shame would cause the men of her family shame too, since it implies that her male relatives are too weak to control her. With regard to hair, a modest Muslim woman would not wear long hair loose but would have it tied back. Today many women wear a headscarf or *hijab* as a sign of their modesty and also of their Islamic identity.

How a person dresses in Muslim outreach is important. For

example, a woman wearing jeans is considered by many Muslims as part of the decadent West, and too short or tight a skirt is considered improper. One basic rule is to show as little of the figure as possible, especially if the husband is around. For a woman, trousers are ideal, and a top should not be tight, short or transparent or have a plunging neckline; ideally it should be loose and long. A Muslim husband might consider your clothes as a factor in deciding whether or not he allows you to visit or have contact with his wife. His greatest fear is that you will be a bad influence on his wife and that she might want to dress like you in Western clothes. For a man in Muslim visitation jeans and a tee-shirt would be considered inappropriate. It is always better to slightly over- than under-dress as this brings respect.

Leave your shoes at the door

When you enter a Muslim home, if you see rows of shoes just inside the door it is good manners to take your shoes off too. Always be prepared to do this (wear socks without holes!) if visiting a Muslim home. Bare feet are very acceptable.

Carry a Bible when you visit a Muslim home

It is a good principle to carry a Bible in a bag on all visits as you never know when you might want to use it. The Bible will need to be unmarked and in a new condition, as Muslims believe that to write on any holy book is to desecrate it. What we consider to be aids to study, such as underlining verses and making notes on the page, are regarded as unacceptable.

It is a good principle to carry a Bible in a bag on all visits.

In a Muslim home the Qur'an is wrapped in a special cloth and put on a high shelf. Before it is taken down the hands are washed, and then it is placed carefully on a table, unwrapped and then presented. Muslims believe that holy books should be treated as holy. We are often very careless with our Bibles, throwing them into cupboards with many other things, and also placing them on the floor. There is nothing worse for Muslims than putting a Bible or Qur'an on the floor, as the floor is considered an unclean place. If you visit a Muslim home with a Bible in your bag, and then the bag is put on the floor, the Bible cannot be produced on that visit.

I always remember the time when a Dutch evangelist held a week-long healing campaign in a local church near to us in East London. We took our Muslim friends who were interested to come to these special meetings. One night one of the young men went forward and accepted Christ as his Lord and Saviour. The next evening during the meeting the evangelist took his large Bible and stood on it and said, "I am standing on the promises of God." That night the young man who had accepted Christ the previous evening rejected the Christian faith because of what he saw as desecration of a holy book.

Basic rules in a Muslim home

When you enter a Muslim house you will be taken into a special front room and shown where to sit. You will be given the seat which is furthest from the door, which is the seat of honour. (The one nearest the door is the humblest). If you just go in and sit down you will most likely be asked to change seats; therefore it is wise to wait until you are shown where to sit. The women will sit together and the men will sit together even if husbands and wives are present and even if the people are elderly. If a husband and wife are sitting near to each other they will sit on different pieces of furniture.

Muslim homes often have two sitting rooms. One is furnished very lavishly, situated nearer the front door and set aside for special guests and occasions. Male guests, and female guests if they are strangers, are ushered into this room. There is often another room where the family lives, and to be ushered into this room is an indication of acceptance and friendship. Unknown guests are never left alone, and a child may be left to sit with the person.

When you are seated, there are certain things you need to be aware of if you are a woman. You will have to be careful how you are sitting, making sure that your skirt does not ride above your knees or your legs become wide apart, which would be considered indecent. You must also avoid crossing your legs, as to point the sole of your foot at someone is considered an insult. If you are sitting on the floor you will need to cross your legs or sit with your legs at the side as this will ensure that you do not point the sole of your foot at anyone.

Your hosts will then proceed to offer you a drink and some food, which you will need to accept so as not to be rude. Usually you will not have a choice of drink, as tea will often just be brought, or you could be offered a cold drink. The tea may have been made in a radically different way from ours, perhaps boiled with condensed milk and with spices added. You will also be offered something light such as biscuits, or some form of Muslim sweet, or something they have made. If you are visiting a Muslim family you must always avoid arriving at meal times, as they will feel obliged to feed you, even though they have not provided for you. Your needs will be placed above the needs of the family.

Hospitality is important for Muslims

Hospitality is very important to the Muslim community, and they will readily invite you into their home, where they will give you special food and gifts. As the honoured guest you will be given the best of everything, and their hospitality must be accepted, even though it can be overwhelming. Even an enemy is given hospitality if he asks for it and will be protected as long as he is the guest in the home. It is considered an honour and blessing from God when someone visits their home and becomes an honoured guest, as they believe that to honour a guest brings eternal rewards.

Unexpected guests are always welcomed, and the family will change their plans to accommodate them. They will immediately give their time and attention to the guest and abandon what they were doing or involve the guest in their activity. They would cancel an engagement or take the guest with them, without even announcing the change of plan to their host. This is very different from Western culture.

Guests may be left to eat alone or with their friend, or they might eat with other members of the same sex in the household or even with the whole family. Guests are served first, followed by the male members of the family

Hospitality is very important to the Muslim community, and they will readily invite you into their home.

and then the rest of the family. If the guests are male the women may eat in a separate room.

With all food and drink only the right hand is used. Knives and forks that require both hands are never used unless the family is used to western manners and etiquette. (The left hand is used for unclean tasks such as the toilet.) Generally food is placed in large dishes, and you will be asked to serve yourself, or maybe your host will serve you. It is good manners to take something of each dish, otherwise you might be asked why you did not try one. If you cannot eat it, to leave it on your plate is perfectly acceptable. If you have an empty plate you will be pressed to have more; therefore if you have eaten sufficient it is wise to leave a little on the plate, as the host will always invite you to eat more. In Muslim culture it would be polite to refuse the first offer to show that you are not being greedy. The host would then persuade you to have more, and you would need to show appreciation by having a second offering. In fact, if he asks you only once, it indicates that he does not really want to offer more. To refuse continually might be considered impolite.

Very little conversation takes place at mealtime, as it is considered a time to eat. It is only after the tea and coffee that conversation will take place and you will be able to share. It is possible to leave after tea and coffee is served.

An invitation to a meal can be a very time-consuming activity. With a Muslim family you cannot just stay for the meal and then leave, as this would be considered very rude. An invitation to a meal could mean staying for half a day or

> An invitation to a meal can be a very time-consuming activity.

longer in each other's company. As the honoured guest you can never offer to help with washing up the dishes after a meal, as this would be considered inappropriate.

The difficulties with "thank you"

We are taught from a young age to say "thank you" and are considered rude if we don't. Many Muslim cultures have no concept of "thank you", and the phrase is not used there. Some Muslims believe that saying thank you is merely acknowledging an obligation, and some believe that these words can bring disaster on the recipient through the gift. To say "thank you" would make you subject to another person. So most Muslims express their appreciation in different words, such as "This gift is so helpful."

The giving of gifts

In Muslim culture the giving and receiving of gifts is different from what we would expect. The purpose of the gift is more important than the person who will receive it, and it may put the recipient under an obligation or discharge an obligation. A gift may be given in order to receive a favour or in recognition of service provided. The more important the person the larger in size the gift will need to be. It is the person's choice whether to wrap the gift or not.

When a wrapped gift is given to the person it will be put in a prominent place to show appreciation and will not be opened until after the guest has left. For Muslims it is essential that all the attention be on the guest and not the present. Once a gift is given it now belongs to the family and not to the person to whom it was given. The most senior member of the family may believe that they have the right to it or, if money is short or they already have something similar, could take the decision to sell it. At weddings, however, the present is opened in front of the giver. It is considered that the giver gets more blessing from giving the gift than the person who receives it.

Gifts are given to family members on various occasions. When someone returns from overseas they are expected to bring a gift back for family members. The older members of the family would expect more expensive gifts. In festivals such as Eid new clothes are worn and the children are given gifts of money from their relatives. At engagements, which are very important, money is given to the parents.

Gifts are given to those outside the family to gain religious merit or when someone recovers from an illness to prevent the illness from returning. At the Eid festival money and food can be given either to receive merit or to cancel an obligation, for example, to balance a gift already received.

Gifts of food are commonly given in a dish. It is common practice that when the dish is returned it is filled with food. If it is returned empty, the person remains under an obligation, and the person who gave it gains religious merit.

Flowers as a gift

The giving of flowers can be difficult, as in the Muslim world flowers are seen as a luxury, and as many people are poor, food is seen as more important. Some Muslims, however, do appreciate flowers, the best choice being those that are red and scented. Flowers can be taken if someone is in hospital, but the colour of the flowers needs to be chosen carefully. Yellow flowers should be totally avoided, as that colour is associated with sickness and bad luck. Flowers are never given after a death.

Praying for the sick

When visiting a Muslim home and engaging in conversation it is best to avoid long silences, as these can be very embarrassing for everyone. It is good to develop the gift of conversation. You must also be very careful never to point with a finger but to use the whole hand, as the pointing of a finger is considered to be very rude.

If a member of the family is sick, ask if you can pray for them before you leave. Pray unashamedly for the Lord to heal them and in the name of Jesus. The family is always very pleased to have prayer for a person who is sick. When we were at St Andrew's we would have a healing service once a month instead of our usual evening service, and everyone would file to the front to be prayed for at the end of the service. This was a great attraction for Muslims and those of other faiths.

> If a member of the family is sick, ask if you can pray for them before you leave.

The giving of compliments

In Muslim culture compliments are understood in a completely different way. For example, if you were to compliment a newborn baby by saying how beautiful it was, this could, Muslims believe, bring a curse on it and open the way for disease or death. One health visitor had a very grave experience of this. She complimented the baby the same way we all do. On a subsequent visit she found the baby was sick, and she was being blamed for having invoked the sickness on the baby by complimenting it. It was a hard learning experience.

The spirit world and unseen forces such as the evil eye are

very real to Muslims and an important part of everyday life. For example, when paying compliments to a new baby, Muslims would first begin by calling on Allah. They believe the evil eye, which is jealous, would then have no power over the baby.

The position is very similar with a possession. If you admire something, it means that you have a desire to own it, and they could feel obliged to give it to you. When you admire an object they feel the evil eye has power over them through this possession and that to avert it they must give it away to the person who admires it.

> The spirit world and unseen forces such as the evil eye are very real to Muslims.

How bad news is communicated

Islam is a culture where bad news is not communicated freely. For example a person who is sick must be cushioned from bad news and given hope. The breaking of bad news is very sensitive and is always done very carefully, usually by a close relative; otherwise the blame may be placed on the bearer of the bad news. It is very rare for Muslims to ask a person who is not a relative to break such news.

If a family member is travelling and their relative dies, the person is not told until they arrive home and have the family's support. If a relative in another country is very ill and it is thought they could possibly die, the family living there will suggest that the other relatives should pay a visit. It is not until the relatives arrive that they are told of the impending death of the person.

In some countries widows are not told of the death of their husbands, as no-one will take the responsibility of informing the person. The family would just not speak of the person again, allowing the widow to draw her own conclusions. When a child's mother or father dies, they are often told not that they have died but just that they have gone away.

Blowing your nose

Nasal discharge is considered as unclean as urine. When a person has a cold they will sniff or wipe their nose without blowing it until they can go outside or to the toilet to blow it. It is preferable to spit or blow your nose outside to prevent the house from becoming unclean. During Ramadan many Muslims will spit out their saliva rather than swallowing it to avoid breaking the fast.

Giving hospitality to Muslims

This can be quite a difficult area to grapple with, as it can be hard to return hospitality. When you give a verbal invitation for the first time your Muslim friends might not accept it, and there will need to be some added persuasion. To give an invitation three times is very positive and shows a concern for the person. The invitation will then be accepted to show appreciation even if the person is unable to come. When accepting the invitation your friend might use the word *Inshallah* which means "If God wills".

> When accepting the invitation your friend might use the word *Inshallah* which means "If God wills".

However, your guest may not arrive for many reasons without informing you: he might have had no intention of coming, or relatives could have turned up at his house, or a member of the family might have fallen sick. In some cultures, to come on time would be considered impolite, so if your guests come late you should not be too upset about it.

Pitfalls to avoid in the giving of hospitality

The seating at a meal should be first according to age, then according to professional status, and only then according to other factors.

If you are inviting your Muslim friend to a meal in a Christian home you should just cook your normal food, but you must avoid pork products and wine. It is quite usual for your Muslim friend either to eat very little or refuse food when you return their hospitality. This can be very difficult to understand, as when they provided hospitality the food was lavish and special. (Whether you cook with *halal* meat or not they will still have a problem because they will be unsure of the other ingredients.) They might take a portion of everything that is being served and then just have a taste of each one. This shows that they appreciate the hospitality but they are not hungry. For them to leave food does not necessarily mean that they do not like it.

For meat to be *halal* it must be ritually killed according to Muslim law. This means that the animal is killed by slitting the throat as a Muslim prayer is recited over the animal. Many products such as soap and face cream can be referred to as *halal*; this means that there are no animal products within them from any animal that has not been ritually killed. You may prefer to serve vegetarian food to your Muslim friends to avoid any problems about meat.

Alcohol in any form is forbidden in Islam. There should be no wine added to the cooking or the use of any ingredient that contains wine unless you are very sure that your friend who is coming to dinner will find it acceptable.

Important occasions for visiting a Muslim home without an invitation

Eid and other festivals

The first day of Eid is the most important time for visiting and is a time when all the relatives visit. In Western countries, where extended families are often still in the country of origin, a visit in the afternoon of the first day is always welcomed.

Births, engagements and marriages

These are important events, and your Muslim friends could give you a written invitation to the engagement or wedding, or they could tell you about it verbally. Both bear equal weight. A written invitation could then be followed by a verbal reminder. These events can be very time-consuming: the whole programme seems to progress very slowly, as spending time with those present is considered an important part of the occasion. Leaving early would cause more misunderstanding than not going. On these occasions you would take a gift with you and dress formally.

For a birth you could take some fruit or a gift for the baby. In some places a gift for the baby during the first 40 days could be a problem, as Muslims believe it might bring the "evil eye" on the baby.

When to arrive for a special occasion

There will be a time given for the start of a wedding, engagement or other occasion and you will need to arrive after that time. The more important the person the later they arrive and the earlier they leave. After the most important person has arrived (for example, the bridegroom at a wedding), no more guests are welcome and everyone must stay until this person has left. On arrival you should greet either the bride's family or the groom's family.

> The more important the person the later they arrive and the earlier they leave.

After the wedding gifts of money are given to the bride's father or mother to offset the expenses of the wedding. Between the third and the tenth day after the wedding women visit the bride and give her gifts for the home or clothing for herself.

The Muslim and death

When someone dies the body is immediately washed several times in water by a family member of the same sex and wrapped in two pieces of cloth. The relatives have to be informed straight away, as the body is usually buried within 24 hours. As the family arrives, expressing grief is the correct thing to do, and you will see all the family members crying and wailing, while the women beat their breasts and even throw themselves on the body.

Many Muslims in the West want to be buried in their home village in their country of origin, and in these cases, after the body has been prepared and wrapped, it is placed in a coffin and sent back. However, in many Western countries there are now Muslim cemeteries or areas set aside within cemeteries for Muslim burials. When all the relatives have arrived for the funeral, the male members of the family will accompany the body to the mosque and then the cemetery, while the women will stay at home until after the burial. At the graveside the body is placed facing Mecca and prayers are said. It is after the burial that the women visit the grave.

The family will be in mourning for forty days. On the first three days the Qur'an will be recited in the mosque for the men and in the home for the women. This is the time when it is essential to visit a Muslim home, especially if the family are good friends and you have been informed about the death. You do not need an invitation to call during these three days, but you will need to wear dark, plain clothes, and gifts of food may be taken but not cards or flowers.

At the end of the forty days the family will hold a "wake" for family and friends, and it is not until the meal is finished that the prayers are said on behalf of the deceased. Quite often there will be a memorial day after one year.

Lending of money

In the Muslim community money is perceived in a different way. It is not unusual for your Muslim friend to ask if you can loan him some money. Loaning him money suggests to him that you have no need of it, and therefore he believes there is no obligation to return it. To receive your money back you would have to say that you need it and give the reason. But asking for it back can be very embarrassing, and the friendship may be lost. To maintain the relationship you might have to consider the money lost unless the borrower returns it of his own free will.

Lending of goods

Many Muslims do not have the same concept as Westerners of returning items that they have borrowed. If you wanted something back you would have to ask for it and say how much you needed it. However, this would not apply to some Muslims who have been living in the West for some time and are more conversant with Western ways.

Differences in attitude to openness

One of the main cultural differences which you will face in evangelism and even speaking to Muslims is that whatever you say will not be taken at face value. In some cultures everything is said in black and white and never alluded to in a round-about or hidden way. Muslims on the other hand expect a person to have a hidden agenda, and they will try and work out what it is. The difficulty is that if you hide things in conversation they feel that they cannot trust you, but if you are transparent they could feel that you have a hidden agenda.

> Muslims expect a person to have a hidden agenda.

What do we do? We need to do what the Bible tells us: to speak with openness, honesty and integrity and to try and overcome cultural weaknesses such as this that do not glorify the Lord. We need to think and act as Christ would act.

5

HOW DO WE WIN A MUSLIM FOR CHRIST?

I n the final analysis we can have all the cultural and theological knowledge, all the understanding, and yet not be able to win a Muslim for Christ. Many Muslims come to Christ simply because they are loved into the kingdom of God by Christians showing the love of Christ sincerely and gently, listening patiently and being helpful whenever possible. We also need to take every opportunity to share the Gospel and to say how we found peace and the assurance of knowing that when we die we will go to heaven. In my experience in this area I have found that very few Muslims actually come to Christ through theological debate and interfaith dialogue. However, this is not to decry attempts to understand Muslims and engage with them. Both approaches have a part to play. It is profitable both to have understanding and knowledge and to be aware of the spiritual battle that rages in the heavenly realm over any Muslim who comes to Christ.

In this context we remember the little old lady who witnesses to her next door neighbour with absolutely no knowledge of Islam but who can show Christ's love. I always remember Joseph, who ran the bookshop that was part of the St Andrew's ministry. Joseph was from Burma, and I always remember him as being old. But he won many Muslims to Christ from that bookshop and by breaking every guideline for evangelising Muslims. One of the points he would put to Muslims was "Do you believe Jesus is the Son of God?" Many a time he would have Muslims on their knees crying for salvation. He was used by the Lord in amazing ways because he saw only Christ and desired only to serve him every moment of the day. His passion was Christ.

At the end of the day it is often our testimony that speaks to a Muslim's heart. Our testimony of how we came to Christ is important, but so also is an up-to the minute-testimony of the Lord's workings in our life, of how he helps, guides and leads us in the ordinary, day-to-day tasks of life. This is often what speaks volumes: that Christ is beside and with us in all our trials and tribulations and that He remains ever faithful.

> **At the end of the day it is often our testimony that speaks to a Muslim's heart.**

Share with them how they can know God

Muslims only know about God; they do not know Him. We need to share with Muslims how they can know God through His Son Jesus Christ and how they are able to have a personal relationship with Him. This is something that is very different from Islam. Islam strives to find God and can never reach Him, as He is the unknowable and cannot be found. In Christ they can have a close relationship with Him by the presence of the Holy Spirit in their lives. They will not be aware of who the Holy Spirit is and will need an explanation, that when Jesus left the earth he promised he would send a comforter and teacher, the Holy Spirit, who is the third person of the Trinity. We will have to explain that He is God at work in our lives, that it is He who convicts us when we do something wrong or sin, and that it is He who gives us the assurance of heaven and sins forgiven.

We need to share with Muslims that God is interested in every part of our lives, no matter how small and insignificant the matter seems. God cares because of His great love for each one of us. This is in stark contrast to Islam.

Pray for a supernatural intervention

One very effective prayer is that the Lord will reveal himself to our Muslim friend in whatever way He desires. The Lord is God and He can do whatever he wills. I have seen the Lord answer this prayer. I have known Muslim women have a vision of Christ: one Muslim woman saw Christ walking across the room to her; another saw a vision of Christ appear on the page of the Gospel she was reading. The Lord is able to reveal Himself through visions, through dreams or by other means whereby people know they have met with the living God.

Get a Gospel into the home

If we can get the word of God into a Muslim home then the Lord is able to speak to Muslims as they read it. It is most helpful if we can give them a Gospel, such as Matthew or Luke (which have genealogies), or even a whole New Testament so they can read the life of Jesus. It is wise not to give a complete Bible as they will start at Genesis and probably give up in Leviticus. Scripture portions or tracts are also ideal.

Do a Bible study with your Muslim friend

If your Muslim friend is interested in what you are saying they might be open to having a weekly Bible study with you. This can be very effective, especially with Muslim women during the day when they often feel lonely and without friends. However, it can prove very difficult to take a Muslim woman to meetings in the church even during the day, as she could feel that this is one step too far. A coffee morning in someone's home could be acceptable, and she might like to come. But in the safety of her home and on her own ground she might feel more comfortable to have a Bible study. If her English is very poor the way might be open for you to teach her English (or any other language, for that matter), and this could be done through Bible stories. A man on the other hand would have more freedom to attend a Bible study group.

Take your male friend to a church meeting

If you are a man and your male Muslim friend is open to discuss spiritual issues he might be interested in coming to some event at the church or even to a worship service. This could apply to the whole family if it was an event such as a barbecue or a film or play in a church hall. As we saw above, it would be difficult to invite a Muslim woman to a meeting in a church, but a Muslim man might come if he were really seeking to know God. Wisdom is called for here. Parents could allow a young person to attend a single-sex club such as a boys' table tennis evening or a girls' sewing class. At all church events you need always and unashamedly to end with a Christian epilogue.

The assurance of heaven

This is a very powerful point in evangelism, as Muslims have no assurance that they will go to heaven and just hope that they might get there. To them death can be a fearful experience because of the uncertainty of what really lies ahead. For a woman it is even more serious and fearful as it says in one of the *hadith* (traditions recording what Muhammad said and did) that Muhammad

> **Muslims have no assurance that they will go to heaven.**

looked into hell and saw that it was full of women. She can attain heaven only by complete obedience to her husband and even then is married to him in heaven. And there is no mention of single women in heaven. We need to share with Muslims the promise and assurance of eternal life for those who know Christ and follow Him.

The assurance of answered prayer

Muslims would have no concept of this as they strongly believe that "Allah wills what he wills"; therefore there is no scope for what they believe to be "changing the will of Allah". Testimonies of answered prayer are valuable and can really speak to a Muslim's heart; we can show that our God is interested enough in us to listen to all our petitions, to hear and to answer. God as our Father is intimately involved in our lives through His Son Jesus, who is real, alive and knowable. To Muslims this view of God is remarkable, attractive and beyond their experience and understanding, as it contrasts sharply with Allah, "the unknowable". We need to speak of our experience of the Lord in our day-to-day living and share our hearts with them.

As we have seen above, Muslims do not have the same concept of sin as Christians and therefore do not respond to questions such as "Do you want to have your sins forgiven?" This standard presentation of the Gospel, focused on forgiveness, does not meet their felt need. But they do respond to Jesus' being sent by God to destroy the works of the devil. We find this idea in 1 John 3:8: "The reason the Son of God appeared was to destroy the devil's work." To this they will give their undivided attention.[1]

Commitment to prayer

As the Lord lays our Muslim friends on our heart let us labour in prayer for them, that we might be the means whereby they can find a new life in Christ. Let us pray without ceasing, recognising it is no accident that they have come across our path, but the will of God. Let us share the word of God without fear, with the confidence and assurance that we are being obedient to Christ and His commission to us.

How to bring Muslims to the point where they can accept Christ

Sometimes we can do this with a comment such as "Would you really like to know Jesus and not just about him?" or "Would you like to experience God in your life?" Confronting Muslims with these questions can cause them to think hard and can bring them to the point where they can find and know God through the Lord Jesus Christ. At some point in our relationship, very much under the guidance of the Holy Spirit, we can bring them to a moment of decision.

Another question you can ask is "Do you want to have the assurance that you will go to heaven when you die?" As we have seen above, it is difficult to raise the problem of sin and salvation, as Muslims don't really understand these concepts in the same way that we do. However, when they come face to face with a holy and righteous God they become aware of their sin and their need of salvation.

Accepting Christ is only the beginning

A person's becoming a Christian is only the beginning of a long journey. The person will need to have a copy of the Bible and supervised Bible studies if possible. It is essential that they are taught immediately the doctrines of the Christian faith and begin to understand it in depth. Try to get alongside them and do Bible studies with them at least weekly. With a married woman Bible studies can be done in an early afternoon or whenever possible. Failing this there are Bible study books available in

> Becoming a Christian is only the beginning of a long journey.

Christian bookshops that they can be given. I cannot emphasise enough the importance of this to enable them to stand firm in the faith.

Secret believers

A "secret believer" is a person who on accepting Christ as Lord and Saviour remains within their family and community and doesn't tell them that he or she has become a Christian. However, they do not continue to follow Islam or accept any of the rules, regulations or theology of their previous faith, and they try to meet with other Christian believers.

The question of "secret believers" is very complex, and the position of these people is certainly not ideal, as the scriptures mention public confession of faith as part of Christian discipleship. In Luke 12:8 Jesus says, "I tell you, whoever acknowledges me before men, the Son of Man will also acknowledge him before the angels of God."

However, when Muslims accept Christ into their lives they can be severely persecuted by family and community, and they might decide to keep their new faith hidden. When a married Muslim woman becomes a Christian she will

> When Muslims accept Christ into their lives they can be serverely persecuted by family and community.

generally have to be a secret believer; otherwise her whole family structure will be destroyed, as she will most likely be thrown out of the family. She will, however, still be able to read the Bible and pray at home. For a single girl becoming a Christian can be very hard as she could be thrown out of the family or even killed in an honour killing just for that reason. Women, whether single or married, face terrible difficulties in these situations and the decision what to do has to be theirs. With a man it can be different: he is the head of the family, and in time the whole family could follow Christ. This problem also occurs in Western countries, where we are seeing more and more examples of young men and women having to flee family for their own safety.

There are countries that have the apostasy law of Islam enshrined within the law of the country, which states that Muslims are not permitted to change their religion or leave Islam, the penalty for leaving being death. This is a serious matter of life and death for the convert, and life can be very difficult for them. In some countries converts have to meet in secret; in others they can be part of the confessing church, but although they can worship in the open, the church is persecuted and under pressure.

Extreme forms of contextualisation

Mission to Muslims can be hard, and in some countries it bears little fruit. There is pressure today on missionaries and those in ministry to Muslims to produce results. In the light of this new evangelistic methods have been devised that aim to contextualise the Gospel more effectively in local cultures, that is, to express it more accurately in the language, thought and behaviour of each place.

This is an important topic that we need to grapple with as it can affect people's walk with the Lord and their eternal destiny. Forms of contextualisation that do not compromise the Christian faith in any way can be acceptable and useful. One method, however, recommends that the Muslim who comes to Christ should stay within their community. At first glance this sounds positive. If a Muslim can stay within their community and function within it as a Christian, nothing could be better.

But the method goes on to say that people should do this by continuing to worship at the mosque, saying they are follower of *Isa* or the Muslim Jesus, observing all the Muslim rituals and observances such as praying five times a day, quoting the creed, keeping Ramadan and going on the pilgrimage to Mecca. They are also to acknowledge the authenticity of the Qur'an as an inspired revelation alongside the Bible and to recognise Muhammad as a true prophet alongside the Old Testament prophets.

One difficulty here is that there is no end to a person's former life and no going forward to a new life in Christ. And how can a person still remain part of a religion that everywhere and in all its communications denies that Jesus is the Saviour, and that He is God? The forces of darkness that surround them will be so great that they will pull them back from following Christ. This method also involves the sin of deception and so will not bring the blessing of God.

By continuing at the mosque new Christians will not be in a position to hear the word of God expounded and to have fellowship with believers. And of course the question would be, "Is the person a genuine, born-again Christian, walking with the Lord?" It is not possible to have feet in two camps; it is divided loyalty. If people remain in the mosque their testimony to Christ is not clear, the temptations are too great to compromise and to go back on their decision.

It can be costly to be a Christian

For a person who converts from Islam to Christianity there is often a price to be paid. They can lose their family, inheritance, position in the community, and work. Their commitment is ultimate and the price can be high. It can involve everything they have and are; their desires and their ambitions are all left at the cross of Christ. There are no half-measures. For them as for us we are either for Christ or against Christ.

But maybe we need to see the matter in a different light, the light of eternity. Everything we have and are belongs to the Lord; we are bought with a price; Christ is our life; and eternity is our home. The challenge comes to us: do we want to live the life that God requires of us and is asking us for? Do we have the courage for it? Are we able to say, as the apostle Paul did in Philippians 3:8, "I consider everything a loss compared to the surpassing greatness of knowing Christ Jesus my Lord"? That is the price many converts have to pay. The reward for their faithfulness will be great.

Points that could be raised by your Muslim friend

1. Your Muslim friend might say to you that the Bible has been changed, as Muslim leaders claim that Christians and Jews have corrupted the Bible, and many Muslims take the word of their

imam without question on all issues. But they cannot provide any evidence to support this claim, or explain who corrupted the Bible, when or why. There is no academic support for their accusation.

Or the question could be posed as follows: "Which Bible would you like me to believe? The Authorised Version? The NIV? You Christians have many Bibles, whilst we have only one Qur'an." You can then answer, "Well, which Qur'an would you like me to read? Yusuf Ali, or Pickthall, or Khan?" Their answer will be that these versions explain the meaning of the Qur'an; then we can say that our Bible versions explain the meaning of the Bible. We will have to go on to say that we have an ancient Bible in its original languages and that the English versions are just translations that make the Bible understandable to people in their own language.

> Your Muslim friend might say to you that the Bible has been changed.

Muslims also believe that Allah is the source of both the Bible and the Qur'an. Some Qur'anic verses speak highly of the Torah (Old Testament) and the *Injil* (the Gospels). Yet if these are the word of Allah, and yet Allah failed to protect them from corruption, then he may fail to protect the Qur'an too. So we can point out that the Muslims' attack on the credibility of the Bible is also an attack on the trustworthiness of the Qur'an.

Be ready too to give a simple introduction to the Bible. The Bible consists of two parts. The first 39 books comprise the Jewish Bible or Old Testament. Its first five books, often called the Torah, are associated with the prophet Moses. These are followed by a set of historical books that describe God's dealings with his people over many centuries. After these come the poetic and wisdom books, including the Psalms, some of which are ascribed to the prophet David. Finally there are the prophetic books, including such important prophets as Isaiah, Micah and Zechariah The second part of the Bible is called the New Testament (or in Arabic the

Injil, meaning "good news" or "Gospel") and contains 27 books. Christians accepted these two collections as our holy book and as the word of God. Be prepared to give a Gospel to your friends; ask them to read it and come back to you with questions.

2. Muslims might say that the original, true Gospel is their Gospel of Barnabas, which

Be ready to give a simple introduction to the Bible.

they claim was written by someone called Barnabas who was a disciple of Jesus. This Gospel of Barnabas supports the teaching of Islam, and evidence shows that it was written in the 14th century AD. As well as contradicting many points of the Gospels, it is not familiar with the history, geography and language of the time of Jesus. Muslims scholars have tried to reposition it into the first and second centuries by rewriting it back into history. But there is no mention of any part of the Gospel of Barnabas in the Dead Sea Scrolls, and there is no ancient documentary evidence for it.

PART II

WHAT DO MUSLIMS BELIEVE?

The word "Islam" means "submission" to God and to his will as revealed through Muhammad, and a Muslim is one who submits.

The Qur'an

The Qur'an is the holy book of Islam and is said to have existed eternally, in heaven, in Arabic, on tablets of stone. Arabic is regarded by Muslims as the language of heaven, and speakers of Arabic have a special prestige in the eyes of the Muslim world. Muslims believe that the Qur'an is the actual word of God, dictated word by word to Muhammad in the last 23 years of his life by the angel Gabriel. Even though it is translated into many languages today, translations of the Qur'an do not bear the same weight or authority as the original version in Arabic.

The Qur'an is the same length as the New Testament and is divided into 114 *suras* or chapters. The *suras* are not arranged in chronological order but roughly in order of length, starting with the longest and ending with the shortest. Therefore it is not possible to pick up the Qur'an and immediately understand it, as it is necessary to know the context of each *sura* and when and where it was revealed. Also as the Qur'an is read some verses appear contradictory, and this problem is resolved by the "Law of Abrogation", whereby the later revelation will abrogate, or cancel, the earlier revelation. *Sura* 13:39 says: "Allah doth blot out or confirm what He pleaseth."

The first *sura* of the Qur'an has only seven verses and is the main Muslim prayer, with which they start every prayer and prostration. It is also called the *Al Fatihah* and has a similar importance to that of the Lord's Prayer in Christianity.

1. In the name of Allah, Most Gracious, Most Merciful.
2. Praise be to Allah, The Cherisher and Sustainer of the Worlds;
3. Most Gracious, Most Merciful;
4. Master of the Day of Judgement,
5. Thee do we worship, And Thine aid we seek
6. Show us the straight way,
7. The way of those on whom Thou hast bestowed Thy Grace, Those whose (portion) is not wrath, and who go not astray.

Sura 1:7 refers to the Jews as those with whom Allah is angry and the Christians are those who have gone astray.

The Qur'an is read in conjunction with the second sacred source text of Islam, the six authoritative *hadith* collections, which include thousands of Muhammad's sayings that were passed on by his companions and were collected from 275 to 350 years after his death. The way of life of Muhammad as recounted in the *hadith* is known as the *sunna* and is used as guidance for his followers.

Muslims believe that Muhammad preaches the same message of impending judgement as the prophets of old before him (Adam, Abraham, Moses, David, John the Baptist, Jesus). They

> **Muslims believe that the Qur'an was the final revelation of God to humankind, that it supersedes all earlier revelations, including the *Injil* and the Torah.**

believe that the Qur'an, given to Muhammad, testifies to the authenticity of the Torah (the books of Moses and the prophets), the Psalms of David and the *Injil* (the gospel given to Jesus as originally revealed). *Sura* 5:46 says: "And in their footsteps we sent Jesus the son of Mary, confirming the Law that had come before him. We sent him the Gospel; therein was guidance and light, and confirmation of the Law that had come before him. A guidance and an admonition to those that fear Allah."

Muslims believe that the Qur'an was the final revelation of God to humankind, that it supersedes all earlier revelations, including the *Injil* and the Torah (which they believe were corrupted by Jews and Christians), and that Muhammad is the final prophet or the "Seal of the Prophets". *Sura* 33:40 says: "Muhammad is not the father of any of your men, but (he is) the Messenger of Allah and the Seal of the Prophets. And Allah has full knowledge of all things."

Who was Muhammad?

Muhammad united the Arabs, a people who were at war with each other and split into tribes. He gave them an identity and a purpose by transforming their society and giving them a scripture, the Qur'an, and a new religion, Islam. This was to have far-reaching consequences.

Muhammad was born around 570 AD in Arabia. Muhammad's grandfather was the leader of the Quraysh tribe ruling in Mecca. His father Abdullah died on a business trip when his wife Amina was seven months pregnant. When Muhammad was six years old his mother died on the return trip from Medina, where they had been visiting Muhammad's father's grave. His paternal grandfather became his guardian until he died, when his uncle Abu Talib took over.

Muhammad remained a bachelor longer than most of his contemporaries and worked for a wealthy and powerful businesswoman, Khadija, who had built up a flourishing caravan business. He travelled a lot throughout the Middle East. She proposed to him because she found in him the qualities she most appreciated in a man. She was forty and Muhammad twenty-five when they married. It was her wealth and the allowance she gave him that freed Muhammad to contemplate and later to go around preaching.

It was whilst he was meditating on Mount Hira that he began to fall into trances, and during one of these periods he claimed to have seen the archangel Gabriel, who gave him a message that his wife Khadija convinced him was from God. The figure he saw claimed to be giving him a message for humankind; this message was, however, contrary to that of the Bible.

The Muslim era began on 20 June 622, when, according to Muslim tradition, Muhammad escaped from persecution in Mecca to a place called Yathrib. This episode is called the *hijra* ("flight" or "immigration"). Muhammad later changed the place-name from Yathrib to Medina. The Muslim calendar begins from this date, and it is a lunar calendar with only 354 days in the year. As this is 11 days shorter than the solar year the dates on which Muslim feasts fall will vary every year.

The Five Pillars Of Islam

Muslims have a set of religious duties called "the five pillars of Islam". These are very simple and are compulsory for every Muslim. In early Islam there was a discussion as to whether jihad should be a sixth pillar. Today some Islamists consider that jihad is the sixth pillar.

The confession or the creed

The Muslim's confession of faith is the first pillar of Islam and is called the *shahada*. It is: "I bear witness there is no god but God (Allah), and Muhammad is the messenger of God (Allah)." This Islamic creed is repeated daily in the round of required prayers. It is the conversion prayer, and when recited by non-Muslims in the presence of two witnesses a person becomes a Muslim. In cases of forced conversion, the person is forced to recite the *shahada* and is then considered to have converted to Islam. When a baby is born the imam recites this *shahada* in the baby's ear. The *shahada* is literally proclaimed from the rooftops in Muslim countries as it is part of the call to prayer by the muezzin from the minaret. What is proclaimed from the rooftops is in effect a denial of the divine Sonship and deity of Christ.

Prayer

The second pillar of Islam is prayer. Islam prescribes ritual prayers five times a day, at set times, facing towards Mecca. These prayers are the dawn

Muslims have a set of religious duties called "the five pillars of Islam".

prayer before sunrise, the noon prayer, the late afternoon prayer, the prayer immediately after the sun sets and the prayer after nightfall. The Qur'an gives no details of these; they are all found in the *hadith*. Ritual movements from standing to kneeling to prostration were all part of pagan Arabic culture before Islam.

Prayer at a mosque is announced by the call to prayer from high on the minaret five times a day. The muezzin cries, "Allah is great. I confess there is no god but Allah. I testify that Muhammad is the Apostle of Allah. Come to prayer, come to do good (success)". Early in the morning he calls "Prayer is better than sleep. Allah is great..."

Before prayer the Muslim must carry out a prescribed ceremonial washing called ablutions. There are rules for washing four parts of the body: the face, from the top of the forehead to the chin and as far as each ear; the hands and arms, up to the elbows; a fourth part of the head, rubbed with the wet hand; and the feet, washed up to the ankles. Many Muslims believe that if any of these parts of the body are not washed all the ritual prayers made afterwards are of no value. The Muslim should also be sober and ritually pure from sexual pollution. After having performed the ablutions the worshipper then proceeds to the recitation of the prescribed prayers accompanied by ritual movements. This can be done in either private or public, and it is common in some countries to see Muslim men saying their prayers on the street.

Apart from daily prayers there are united prayers on a Friday that all men are obliged to attend, and it is during this common, public worship that the imam delivers a sermon. In these Friday prayers some mosques have prayers cursing Jews and Christians. Most mosques have a separate room for the women to perform ablutions and pray. A very few progressive mosques accommodate women in the main congregation, but even then in a separate place from the men. Not all mosques have places for women, and so they are required to pray at home.

> Islam does not expect worshippers to develop a relationship with God in prayer.

There is also a tradition called *du'aa*, which is another form of calling upon God that could be considered as more like extemporary praying. However many of these *du'aa* traditions are only a repetition of prayers instituted by Muhammad. More mystical experiences take place within the Sufi tradition, which was developed after Muhammad's death.

Islam does not expect worshippers to develop a relationship with God in prayer; it is more an act of obligatory duty. In Christianity there is a wide diversity of prayer, from structured, liturgical prayer to more extemporary prayers. Prayer for the Christian is more than a series of ritual movements and set prayers as it is built on a personal relationship between the individual and God. Christian prayer is entry into the presence of God through Jesus Christ as the mediator. Christians can pray at any time and in any circumstance and have the confidence that God hears and answers. There are many types of prayer: personal prayer, intercessory prayer (for others), prayers of adoration, prayers for healing and sacramental prayers, to name a few.

Giving of alms

The third pillar of Islam is the giving of alms. In Islam two terms are used for almsgiving. One is *zakat*, which refers to the legal obligation of every Muslim; the other is *sadaqa*, which denotes the voluntary offerings made at *eid-ul-fitr*, the annual festival at the end of Ramadan.

Every adult Muslim must give *zakat* in proportion to the property owned, as long as they have sufficient money for their own subsistence. In Sunni Islam the rate is 2.5 percent. *Zakat* is given to the poor and needy, those in debt, travellers, those who administer the funds and recent converts to Islam. They can also be used for the "cause of Allah", a phrase that denotes jihad (among other things). In Islam prayer and alms-giving are considered inseparable, and it is said that alms-giving seals prayer.

Fasting

The fourth pillar of Islam is fasting. Fasting takes place during the month of Ramadan every year. This is the ninth month of the Muslim calendar and the time when Muslims believe that the angel Gabriel first revealed the Qur'an to Muhammad. Ramadan is announced when one trustworthy witness testifies before the authorities that the new moon has been sighted. A cloudy sky may therefore delay or prolong the fast.

Muslims teach that the significance of Ramadan is that humans have larger needs than bread and that their bodies are to be their servants and not their masters. Great self-discipline is shown by those Muslims who take it seriously, as they do not even swallow their saliva. Another purpose of Ramadan is to show sympathy with the poor and destitute.

Fasting is defined as abstinence from food and drink, smoking and sexual intercourse during the hours between sunrise and sunset. During the month of Ramadan the family gets up early, before the sun has risen, and has a large meal. After the sun has set the fast is broken, often with dates, and then there is exuberant feasting every night until very late. It is said that the joy of feasting increases every night and reaches its peak on the 30th day of Ramadan, which is the final day of the fast and is called the *eid-ul-fitr*. There is more food consumed during the month of fasting than in any other month of the year.

> Fasting is defined as abstinence from food and drink, smoking and sexual intercourse during the hours between sunrise and sunset.

Fasting is compulsory for the Muslim, except for young children and the mentally disabled. Those who are sick, travelling, pregnant, nursing mothers or having their period are able to postpone their fast for a later date. This change of daily habits demands a high measure of personal will-power and self-discipline, and is less difficult in countries where everyone is doing the same.

As with prayer, Christians have no prescribed way of fasting. It is still very much a ritual of the Eastern Church, where fasting takes place every Wednesday and Friday and is a vegan fast, in which no animal or fish products are eaten. Eastern Christians also fast during Lent for 50 days and on various other days throughout the year, where fasting is from food and drink for a period of time. The person is able to choose the length of time of their fast, but it is always followed by a Eucharist and then a vegan meal. It differs from Ramadan in that the period of time is longer and it is not followed by feasting but by a simple meal.

The *hajj*

The fifth pillar of Islam is the *hajj* or the pilgrimage to Mecca in Saudi Arabia, where Muslims perform the *hajj* rituals around the Islamic shrine, the *Ka'ba*. This takes place in the twelfth month of the Muslim calendar. The pilgrimage is obligatory once in a lifetime for those who can afford it, some traditions permitting the sending of a substitute even posthumously.

Various rituals are performed, some of which were adopted by Muhammad from those performed by the idol-worshipping religions of the Arabian Peninsula hundreds of years before. They include going around the *Ka'ba* seven times as Muslims believe that this is the place where Abraham offered his son Ishmael for sacrifice and then God provided a substitute animal. (It must be noted here that Christians believe that Abraham offered up his son Isaac, and not Ishmael.)

This pilgrimage usually has a great effect on Muslims, and on returning they are religiously revived and consider themselves new men and women. They believe that they have had all their sins washed away and some even say that they have become "born anew".

It must be remembered that it is extremely difficult within Islam to criticise or analyse the system of theology and beliefs. Everything must be accepted blindly. Although there are Muslim scholars who talk about reforming Islam, they are condemned as apostates by other parts of the Muslim community. Those who are considered blasphemous, such as author Salman Rushdie, risk losing their lives.

ISLAM AND SPIRITUAL WARFARE

S ome say that Christianity and Islam have much in common and that they are blood brothers. But on a close analysis the two religions are found to be poles apart; the divide between them is so great that it can never be bridged. The centre of their opposition remains the deity of Christ, His status as Son of God, and the cross.

It is essential to understand the Muslim attitude to the cross

Muslims do not believe that Jesus died on the cross or rose from the dead but think that He was raised to heaven alive without death. Thus the very central doctrines of the Christian faith are denied by Islam. To them Jesus is not the Son of God but is just a mere man and a prophet of Allah like the other prophets before him, who have all been superseded by Muhammad, the final prophet. 1 John 2:22 says, "Who is the liar? It is the man who denies that Jesus is the Christ. Such a man is the antichrist: he denies the Father and the Son."

For Christians the cross is the centre of all revelation and became the symbol of sacrificial love, redemption, mercy and compassion. Christ is the conqueror whose victories have been won through loss, humiliation and suffering, and it is because of His death on the Cross that we have the forgiveness of sin and the certain hope of eternal life.

The words "the cross" do not appear in the Qur'an, although

related words such as "crucifixion" are found there. However, a denial of the crucifixion is hinted at in the Qur'an 4:157: "They killed him not nor crucified him, but so it was made to appear to them."

Muhammad had such a repugnance to the very form of the cross that he destroyed everything that was brought into his house with the cross on it.[1] The Muslim attitude to the cross is not just one of denial and neutrality, but one of intense hatred and opposition. I remember when travelling around Turkish Northern Cyprus coming across a church that was standing empty and derelict with the altar area desecrated, and in a shed at the back were all the crosses, smashed.

In Muslim eschatology Jesus will come again, but he will come as the Muslim Jesus or 'Isa. One of the first things 'Isa will do will be to destroy all crosses, or in other words eradicate Christianity from the earth. This opposition to the cross is very intense. We read in Colossians 2:15: "And having disarmed the powers and authorities, he made a public spectacle of them, triumphing over them by the cross."

The cross is the pivotal point of spiritual warfare

The cross is the pivotal point of spiritual warfare, as it is the place where Satan and all the demonic powers are defeated by the blood of Christ. This is why they have such a hatred for the cross. We see a similar hatred in Islam.

> **The cross is the pivotal point of spiritual warfare.**

The cross is a very powerful symbol for Christians in the Muslim world today. It is the symbol that brings persecution and suffering to the Church. Egyptian Christians unashamedly tattoo the cross on their forearms to declare that they are Christians and suffer persecution because of it. Young girls wear a cross at universities and colleges and can be failed in their exams because of it. In Malaysia no new church is permitted to have a cross on it. In the context of Islam we can see clearly what is meant by the offence of the cross as described in 1 Corinthians 1:18: "For the message of the cross is foolishness to those who are perishing, but to us who are being saved it is the power of God."

We are in a spiritual battle whether we like it or not

In everyday life, and even more so in the context of ministry, we must remember that we are in a spiritual battle. The forces of darkness are arrayed against us, and as we embark on any form of ministry we are entering a battlefield that continues in the heavenly realm between Christ and Satan, the powers of darkness and the powers of light. Ephesians 6:12 says: "For our struggle is not against flesh and blood, but against the rulers, against the authorities, against the powers of this dark world and against the spiritual forces of evil in the heavenly realm."

We must always be aware of the ways and workings of the Evil One, or in other words we must know our enemy to be able to defeat him. We cannot ever in the Christian walk be ignorant of Satan's devices or just wish to distance ourselves from him. He stalks us even more as we seek to bring people from the kingdom of darkness to the kingdom of light. In James 4:7 we read: "Resist the devil, and he will flee from you."

What we read about here is active not passive; we resist the devil and evil forces actively by prayer and as we resist, the devil has to leave defeated.

In Ephesians 6:11 we are told: "Put on the full armour of God so that you can take your stand against the devil's scheme," To be able to stand against the devil's wiles requires taking up the full armour of God, which should be part of the normal Christian walk. If one has protection against the enemy one is able to have victory over him.

Folk Islam

In Islam we encounter a religion every aspect of which is laid out in detail, a religion that in its basic form is simple to understand and follow, with all its rules and regulations. However, there is another side to Islam, which remains hidden but is just as important. This is the world of folk Islam or the outworking of popular Islam in the lives of people, with its angels and demons, *jinn*, cursing and the evil eye. These are not questioned but are accepted as part of normal everyday life; indeed, they are an integral part of Islam as defined by the Qur'an. In the West the question arises: do we actually believe that this realm of demons and spiritual powers exists? We certainly find it in the Bible.

> There is another side to Islam, which remains hidden. This is the world of folk Islam.

Demons or evil spirits in the Old Testament

Whilst the activity of demons and demon possession are not prominent in the Old Testament, they are however a constant reality. The Old Testament contains clear references to Satan, demons and their influence upon humans. With every decline in the spiritual life of Israel there was a corresponding increase in idolatry, demon-worship and the associated occult practices of Israel's neighbours. The Israelites were constantly warned by God not to become involved with their heathen neighbours and take on their religions and practices. The Old Testament contains warnings against mediums and those practising spiritism, those engaging in witchcraft and the casting of spells or curses (Deuteronomy 18:9-12). Again in the book of Deuteronomy (32:17) we see that heathen gods were considered to be demons, and behind every idol was a demonic power. Paul also says in 1 Corinthians 10:19-20 that those who sacrifice to idols sacrifice to demons.

One well known appearance of Satan in the Old Testament is in the book of Job, where he gets permission from the Lord to test Job.

In Job 1:12 the Lord says to Satan: "Very well then, everything he has is in your hands, but on the man himself do not lay a finger".

And Zechariah 3:1-2 says: "Then he showed me Joshua the high priest standing before the angel of the Lord, and Satan standing at his right side to accuse him. The Lord said to Satan, "The Lord rebuke you, Satan! The Lord who has chosen Jerusalem, rebuke you! Is not this man a burning stick snatched from the fire?"

David was enlisted in Saul's court to play the harp because Saul was tormented by an evil spirit. In 1 Samuel 16:14 we read, "Now the Spirit of the Lord had departed from Saul, and an evil spirit from the Lord tormented him." However the story of Saul shows that he was responsible for the evil that came upon him. (1 Samuel 13:8-14)

Demons or evil spirits in the New Testament

In the New Testament we are confronted straight away with demons, the physical manifestations of demonic possession, and Jesus casting out demons. The conflict with the forces of evil is mentioned some fifty times in the Gospels alone. We see Jesus curing many who had diseases, sicknesses and evil spirits (Luke 7:21) and healing a demon-possessed man who was blind and mute (Matthew 12:22-23). A woman with a spirit of infirmity had been crippled for eighteen years and was bent over (Luke 13:10-13), and a slave girl had a spirit by which she predicted the future (Acts 16:16-18).

I remember when I entered Christian ministry I gave very little thought to this realm, until one day a church member visited me to share her problems. They seemed so immense and complex that I naively said to her "I think I need to pray for you". I put my hands on her head and prayed, and (much to my horror) she collapsed on the floor, and there were strange voices coming from her. I worked out that these must be demons, so I continued to pray. After several hours I seemed to be making no headway, and strange things were happening that dumbfounded me. I rang the local Anglican vicar, who was part of the charismatic movement, and sought his help. He told us to come round, and as we sat in his vestry he read the appropriate passage for exorcism from the prayer book. She immediately took off out of the vestry at high speed and went screaming down the road. I ran off after her and brought her back home. It was getting late by now, so she stayed overnight, and I have to admit that I hid all the kitchen knives. It was all very worrying. The next day I had to try to seek other help, as the situation was getting so desperate. I was recommended to go and see an Anglican vicar in south London. I drove her there and, much to my relief, he knew exactly what to do. After several hours of praying she was free and a changed person. The Lord was beginning to open my eyes to a new realm, one in which I had known about only in the pages of the Bible. Now it was a reality, and I was being equipped for a ministry to the Muslim community.

Angels in Islam

Angels live in what Muslims consider to be the other world. In Islam there are seven heavens, which Muslims believe exist one above the other,[2] with the throne of God being above the highest heaven. The angels occupy places in all the heavens but are arranged in order of rank.[3] They believe that the highest ranking angels are around the throne of God singing praises and interceding for humankind.

In Islam there are two angels, called Harut and Marut, who teach magic to people. The Qur'an teaches that magic powers were revealed by Allah to these two angels at Babylon. They were then sent down to earth by Allah to teach magic to humankind. When Harut and Murat reveal the magic to someone they are to warn the person that it will bring them no benefit, only disbelief, and they are to harm no-one with it except by the permission of Allah.[4]

Jinn and *Iblis*

In Islam there are categories of demons or evil spirits. There are *jinn* (which have the characteristics of demons) and more vicious evil spirits called Shaytans. As Christians we do not distinguish between types of demonic powers, as we believe that they are all emissaries of Satan.

The Qur'an says that *jinn* or *jinni* are beings that were created by Allah from smokeless fire before the creation of man[5]. Smokeless fire is the name for the tips of the flames, which are considered to be the purest and the best of the fire. The Qur'an goes on to say that both *jinn* and humans were created by Allah to serve him[6] and that the Qur'an was sent for both of them[7].

Muslims believe that *jinn* are part of the spirit world somewhere between humans and angels, whose abode is within the human domain rather than the heavenly domain. The *jinn* have power and capabilities that are beyond those of humans, but they share with humans certain qualities such as intellect, freedom and the power to choose between true and false, right and wrong, good and bad[8]. *Jinn* form an important component in folk Islam, and some illnesses, medical conditions and even death are attributed to them. For example, some believe that whooping cough can be caused by *jinn*'s tickling a child's lungs, and someone who has an epileptic fit is believed to be possessed. Muslims believe that death can also be caused by *jinn*.

> **Muslims believe that *jinn* are part of the spirit world somewhere between humans and angels.**

In the Qur'an *Iblis* was the first *jinn* recorded as disobedient[9]. *Iblis* is considered to be the proper name for Satan. In Islam angels were created by Allah from light and *jinn* were created from smokeless fire, and therefore these are their origins, as humans' origin (Muslims believe) is clay[10]. The throne of *Iblis* is considered to be on the sea, and it is from there he sends forth his armies of *jinn*. The nearer the *jinn* to him, the greater its sedition.

The Biblical origins of Satan and evil spirits

The Bible says that angels, like humans, were created by God. There was a time when angels did not exist, only the triune God, as we read in Colossians 1:16: "For by him all things were created: things in heaven and on earth, visible and invisible, whether thrones or powers or rulers or authorities; all things were created by him and for him."

> The Bible says that angels, like humans, were created by God.

In Hebrews (1:14) angels are called "ministering spirits". They are essentially spiritual beings but can take on bodily form when God appoints them to special tasks. When the women went to the tomb of Jesus early on the resurrection morning they saw there an angel in the form of a young man. We read in the Gospel of Mark (16:5): "As they entered the tomb, they saw a young man dressed in a white robe sitting on the right side."

Scripture speaks of good and bad angels, of holy angels and those who sinned and did not keep their first position or position of authority (Jude 6). These fallen angels are now part of the demonic realm with Satan. Satan, who was known as Lucifer, was the chief amongst the angels created to have dominion over the earth and was called the "son of the morning" (Isaiah 14:12). He was the most beautiful of all the created beings in heaven and was covered with precious stones and gold (Ezekiel 28 11-19). However, his beauty caused him to become proud, and sin entered as he desired to be as God and to have the supreme authority. In Ezekiel 28:17 it says: "Your heart became proud on account of your beauty and you corrupted your wisdom because of your splendour. So I threw you to the earth."

When God cast Lucifer out of heaven with all his followers (the fallen angels) he became known as Satan, which in Hebrew means "opposer, adversary, enemy". The fallen angels form the army of

Satan or the forces of darkness, whose aim is to destroy the works of God. They ceaselessly oppose God and strive to deflect his will.

Jinn in relation to humankind

Jinn are responsible for their actions. As proof of this Muslims cite the instances where the Qur'an censures and curses the *jinn* and mentions the punishment that Allah has prepared for them. The obligations of the *jinn* are not the same as the obligations of humans, as they are different from humankind in constitution and experience. They are similar to humankind in being bound by commands and prohibitions, the *halal* and the *haram*[11], but what they are commanded and forbidden is different from what applies to humans. According to the *hadith* there are three types of *jinn*. One type consists of snakes and dogs; the second has wings and flies; and the third travels about[12].

Jinn are considered to be invisible to humankind but are able to assume what forms and shapes they please, and when their form becomes condensed they become visible. They appear most commonly in the shape of snakes, dogs, cats, scorpions and human beings[13].They can be either good or evil[14].

If the *jinn* are considered to be good they appear as very handsome men or very beautiful women. If evil they are horribly hideous. They are more often considered to be evil rather than good, and they have different names according to their degree of evilness. *Shaytan* is the name used for *jinn* who are malicious and who have become wicked; an *ifrit* is stronger and more powerful than a *shaytan*[15].

Muslim attitudes towards dogs

In most schools of Islamic law dogs are classed as ritually unclean. This means that Muslims may not pray after being touched by a dog. If they happen to be touched by dog saliva they must wash the "affected" area seven times before being considered pure again[16]. Muslims also believe that a dog could be *jinn*. All this explains the

Muslims' attitude and fear towards dogs. They keep as far away from dogs as possible, and if they encounter one they will desperately try to ignore it and not to provoke it in any way, as they believe that otherwise *jinn* could possess them or afflict them with sickness or death.

> **If we have a dog we must keep it completely out of sight if we are going to invite Muslims into our home.**

If we have a dog we must keep it completely out of sight if we are going to invite Muslims into our home.

Further characteristics of *jinn*

Jinn marry and have children. Qur'an 55:56 says: "Whom no man or jinn before them hath touched." This *sura* (verse) is taken to indicate that *jinn* have intercourse. As *jinn* have to die they marry for the sake of having children and the continuity of *jinn*. It also says in the *sunna* that *jinn* reproduce as the children of Adam reproduce[17].

Jinn eat and drink. Their food is bones and dung, and they live in houses, graveyards, ruins, deserts, bathrooms and dark places and even keep pets. *Jinn* are frequently found in markets and other places of mischief and corruption. It is because of the presence and impurity of *jinn* that it is forbidden for Muslims to pray in bathrooms and graveyards. Jinn are most frequently present at nightfall[18] and can spend the night in a person's nose.

Jinn can be either Muslim or non-Muslim. Muslim scholars agree that Muhammad was sent by Allah to both *jinn* and humans. In the Qur'an (46:29-32) is considered to be absolute proof of the universality of the message for both humans and *jinn*[19]. There are religions and sects amongst the *jinn*. The non-Muslim *jinn* are defined as those who have refused to accept Islam and have as a result developed different ways of life and different religions. When they die those who disbelieve will enter the fire, and those who believe will enter the garden or Paradise[20].

Jinn and humans can intermarry. This may seem to be so far-fetched as to be unbelievable, but Muslims believe that marriage between men or women and *jinn* can take place. In Qur'an 17:64 it says: "...mutually share with them wealth and children..."

For example, *jinn* can appear to a man as a beautiful woman, and she will seduce him and have sexual intercourse with him. He will then be bound to her and become her slave forever. The man may marry this *jinn* and remain faithful to her rather than to his wife. Some Islamic scholars do say that this type of marriage is forbidden in Islam.

> It is because of the presence and impurity of *jinn* that it is forbidden for Muslims to pray in bathrooms and graveyards.

There are many stories like the following: "After we had passed Ilbira, the rain forced us to take shelter, so we went to sleep in a cave. There was a group of us. While I was asleep something awakened me. I woke up and there was a woman surrounded by some other women. She had one eye fixed open. I was alarmed. She said, 'Don't be afraid. I have come to marry you to one of my daughters who is like the moon'. I replied out of my fear of her. 'By the choice of Allah'. I looked again and some men had appeared. They looked like the woman who had come to me with their eyes fixed open. They appeared to be a Qadi and witnesses. The Qadi performed the engagement and marriage contract and I accepted. Then they got up. The woman returned with a beautiful girl whose eye, however, was like that of her mother. She left her with me and departed. My fear and distaste increased. I began to throw stones at the people about me so as to wake them up. When one of them finally woke up, I began to offer supplications. Then it was time to depart and we set off. The young girl did not leave me. This state of things went on for three days. On the fourth day the woman came to me and said, "It seems that you do not like this young girl and want to part from her". I said, "Yes, by Allah!" She said, "You have divorced her". Then she left and I did not see her again[21].

There are instances, though rare, when a woman may be captured by male *jinn*.

Having a relationship with *jinn*

Muslims believe that if a *jinn* takes a liking to a person it will follow him or her around, and if the person is fearful the *jinn* will become more active. However, if the person ignores the *jinn* it will go away. Again this can seem to be unbelievable, but this subject is serious, and these things do appear to happen. As Christians we need to realise that here we are in the realm of demonic powers. Such a person will be bound to the *jinn* (whoever this *jinn* or demon masquerades as) by demonic powers and will be unable to free themselves unless they are released by the power of Christ. When a person forms a relationship with a *jinn* it is described as being "struck by *jinn*", and can manifest itself as an illness or total possession of the person. There are named *jinn*, which people fear most, and which they believe cause sickness, paralysis and death.

In dealing with the problems caused by *jinn*, Muslims will obtain a diagnosis made by a practitioner using divination or a medium-induced trance. A practitioner of some power is required, and his services tend to be expensive. He may sleep with part of the afflicted person's clothing and in the morning announce the solution that came to him in a dream, or the practitioner may have a personal *jinn* that aids him in the diagnosis. All this can be very costly, and sometimes a cure may not be found, and in these cases strong charms are used to reduce the symptoms or prevent a recurrence of the attack. Sometimes the cure is found by forming a symbiotic relationship between the afflicting spirit and the afflicted person[22].

Muslims fear *jinn* and will do anything to avoid encountering them as they believe their purpose is to seek, harm or destroy them in some way. When Muslims enter a lavatory or go to bed they have to pray, "O Allah I seek refuge with you from the male and female Shaytans [more vicious evil spirits][23]." They also believe that Shaytan is present when a man has intercourse with his wife, and the man must mention Allah and seek refuge from Shaytan, otherwise the Shaytan will have intercourse along with him. When a man has intercourse with his wife whilst she is menstruating the Shaytan precedes him, and she conceives and brings forth a

> **Muslims fear *jinn* and will do anything to avoid encountering them.**

child of the *jinn*[24]. Muslims believe that Shaytan are present when a child is born and will prick it and cause it to yell[25].

How Muslims cope with *jinn* and Shaytan

How do Muslims cope with *jinn* and what measures do they have to take to protect themselves from the activity of *jinn*?

Muslims take refuge from *jinn* by quoting Qur'an 16:98-99: "When thou doest read the Qur'an seek Allah's protection from Satan the Rejected one. No authority has he over those who believe and put their trust in their Lord." As we have seen above, they have to do this constantly.

Certain verses are considered better than others for protection from *jinn*. For example, in Qur'an 113 (called the *Al Falaq*) it says: "This sura provides the antidote to superstition and fear by teaching Muslims to seek refuge for Allah from every kind of ill arising from outer nature and from dark and evil plotting and envy on the part of others." From *sura* 113:1 they quote: "I seek refuge with the Lord of the Dawn." Or they might quote the Bismallah (Qur'an 1:1), "In the name of Allah, Most Gracious, Most Merciful."

When a Muslim goes to the toilet he will cough and repeat one of these protective formulae to warn the *jinn* that he is coming. If he fails to do this he could be attacked from a spirit of the toilet.

Another method of protection is to constantly remember or think of Allah. Another is to recite the last two verses of the Sura Al-Baqarah. Muslims believe that Shaytan will not come near a house in which these are recited for three nights. And there are many other precautionary measures that Muslims can take, such as ensuring that they pray five times a day, refrain from excess in food, socialising, speech and so on[26].

The evil eye and envy

The concept of the evil eye in Islam is that both people and anything that is precious to them are vulnerable to hurt or destruction simply by a person's envy. This envy or jealousy comes through the eye and is seen as a tangible force. Muslims consider envy to be one of the evil forces of the unseen that can affect a person adversely and are the major cause of crises in their lives. Evil forces are considered to come from a person who envies and to injure the life of the other person. It is because the evil eye is conveyed by a look that it is so insidious. Muslims say, however, that the harmful rays come only from the envier in states of malice, but that everyone can have spiteful, grudging impulses from time to time.

> The concept of the evil eye in Islam is that both people and anything that is precious to them are vulnerable to hurt or destruction simply by a person's envy.

Muslims believe that there are two types of evil eye: one is the human and the other *jinn*. There is a sound *hadith* that says that Muhammad saw a slave-girl in her house with yellowness in her face and commanded a spell to be used. She had been afflicted by the evil eye[27]. Muslims believe that envy and magic are both amongst the evils that cannot be seen but are yet on a par with visible evils.

To us being envious of a person would be considered as one of the emotions that are common to humanity and not a force in its own right. The person it affects mainly is the one who is envious, as it can lead to jealousy and hatred, which can seriously affect that person's life. If they are consumed by envy it can also lead to sin before God. We have an example of this in the Old Testament, in 1 Samuel 18:9-10: "And from that time on Saul keep a jealous eye on David. The next day an evil spirit from God came forcefully upon Saul."

Saul had such an intense jealousy of David that evil entered into him, and he tried to destroy David. Saul was in reality destroying himself. Envy was not an outside force or an evil eye trying to destroy David but evil that came from Saul himself. The tables are reversed as Saul becomes fearful of David. It says in 1 Samuel 18:12: "Saul was afraid of David, because the Lord was with David but had left Saul."

To deflect the evil eye or to control *jinn*, talismans or amulets are used. A verse of the Qur'an is written on a scrap of paper, and this will be sewn into a pouch and placed on a part of the body. However, after all these precautions a Muslim will still try to avoid places that he believes have dangerous supernatural inhabitants.

How to receive *Baraka* or blessing

The opposite to the negative force of the evil eye is a positive magic force or blessing known as *Baraka*. It resides with saints or holy people, who are in various locations where people are able to visit them. This *Baraka* can also be with objects and is generally received by some form of touch.

For most Muslims saints and shrines play an important part in their view of life. There are both living and dead saints in the Muslim world. In India, Pakistan, Bangladesh and the continent of Africa it is mainly the dead saints that are venerated at shrines. Saints that are living (*pirs*) are visited

> For most Muslims saints and shrines play an important part in their view of life.

by people for healing, intercession, guidance or to bestow *Baraka*.

Alive or dead, saints are believed to possess great power. The kind of miracles (*karama*) attributed to them include raising the dead, walking on water, covering great distances in short times, healing, having knowledge of the future, guarding people or tribes and being in two places at one time. Shaykh Zuwayyid, one of several saints venerated among the Bedouin of Sinai, is reputed to have filled a food bowl simply by looking at it[28].

We see from all this that Muslims are bound by fear and superstition and their lives are ruled by it. For them the spirit world is as real as the physical world. What they need is a release from it and to find a new freedom that comes only through knowing Christ.

The Night of Power

Qur'an 97 1-5 reads: "We have indeed revealed this (message) in the Night of Power. And what will explain to thee what the Night of Power is? The Night of Power is better than a thousand months. Therein come down the angels and the Spirit by Allah's permission on every errand. Peace... This until the rise of Morn."

For every Muslim this is a very important night. The Night of Power occurs during Ramadan, and Muslims believe it to be the night that marked the beginning of the revelation of the Qur'an to Muhammad and his mission of delivering it to humankind. They believe that there was a descent of the angels, and that the Spirit (Gabriel) with the permission of their Lord carried the Qur'an. Some say that it is on the 27th night of Ramadan, others on the 21st, and some others say no more than that it is in Ramadan[29].

It is a night, Muslims believe, when the heavens are open and Gabriel and the angels descend and pray for mercy for everyone they find in worship. Any duty, such as reciting the Qur'an, is better done on this night than in a thousand months. (A thousand months can be understood as a large number.) It is also a night when all previous sins can be forgiven. It is considered a night of safety from any wrongdoing or mischief, but it can be a night of much violence against Christians.

When a Muslim is born

I always think of Muslims as having Islam engrained on their soul. It all starts when a woman is pregnant. She will visit a holy man or imam and will be given verses of the Qur'an to drink. The verses are written in a special ink and then washed into a glass with water, which she drinks. When the baby is born the imam immediately visits the family and shouts the *Shahada* (or conversion prayer) into the baby's ear: "There is no god but God and Muhammad is the messenger of God."

This act binds the baby to Islam by spiritual forces and ensures that there is continuity in the faith. When Muslims come to Christ they often say that this act of binding at birth has been a barrier to their accepting Christ. When a Muslim does come to Christ we will need to pray for them that they will be freed from the spiritual forces of Islam by the name and power of Christ. If this prayer for release is not made they often do not grow in the Christian faith as well as we would hope. In many parts of the world, when a Muslim comes to Christ this prayer is included as part of the prayer to receive Christ into their lives.

Cursing is a part of Folk Islam

Cursing is an integral component of folk Islam. A curse is a concentration of evil that is levelled against a person or persons by invoking the powers of the occult. It can be performed by an individual or by visiting a practitioner who has the occult powers or access to them. In Muslim newspapers even in the West there are advertisements for such services. I remember seeing them in East London Muslim newspapers, in which practitioners advise wives to seek their services to ensure that their husband does not go off with another woman.

Cursing is an integral component of folk Islam.

It was some years ago that a leader in one of the largest mosques in Europe came to visit us. Sitting in our lounge in the middle of East London he informed us that he had a curse placed on him and asked if we were able to remove it. This curse had afflicted him for 25 years. We counselled him that it could easily be removed by the power of the risen Christ, but afterwards the demon would come back if he did not accept Christ into his life. We were able to share the Gospel and the way of salvation. After many hours he went away sorrowful as the price of freedom from the curse was too high.

Many mosques have prayers of cursing against Christians and Jews every Friday and these are sometimes even uttered in public over the loudspeaker. We need to be aware that in some parts of the world there are all-night prayer meetings for the cursing of Christians and Jews and also that Christians will be divided amongst themselves.

How to get freedom from a curse

We must not underestimate the power of cursing and the effect it can have on a person. Christians are protected by the Lord from evil forces, but there are instances when a curse has been put on a Christian and it begins to have an effect on the person's life. For this to happen there always has to be a definite act of occult powers against the person, and it is certainly not an everyday occurrence. The person who has been cursed will always know that something is wrong, but it can be very difficult to go for help when their theology denies the possibility of what has happened. Also it is very difficult for the person to admit that there is a problem in this area, as they will naturally want to attribute it to every other cause. That is exactly what Satan would want.

How to tell if a Christian has a curse placed on them

The chief target of Satan's attack is the mind. This is why in Ephesians 4:23 we are exhorted to have a renewed mind or the mind of Christ. The person who is afflicted will at times feel as though they are literally in hell and will have great difficulty in reading the Bible, praying and attending church. The forces of evil will at times almost seem too strong to cope with. However alongside this there will be periods when this attack appears to have finished completely and everything returns to normal. The person may then believe that they have been healed and the problem will never recur. But unless there is a definite act of removing the curse the spiritual conflict and agony of soul will return at some later date.

The curse usually happens as the result of a conflict with a person who has occult powers and a deep-seated hatred for Christianity. Or it could be someone who took exception to evangelism, feeling it was upsetting their community, or who had some other grievance against the person or was jealous, and who either activated the curse in person or went to someone who specialises in this field. Or, maybe the person activating the curse just could not stand the presence of Jesus the Christ, his death and resurrection, and the demonic powers within were activated against a Christian, who represents Christ and has received the Holy Spirit. This can happen to missionaries in Muslim evangelism, as shown by the large failure rate and the disasters that beset many of their lives. In Muslim evangelism we need to be very aware of the spiritual battle that rages around us, to be watchful and diligent and never to dismiss this area of ministry.

> In Muslim evangelism we need to be very aware of the spiritual battle that rages around us.

Removal of a curse

A curse is not difficult to remove, but the source must be identified if at all possible. Cursing and demonic powers can usually be traced back to a source, which is something quite definite and quantifiable. The person, on reflecting, will be able to identify a point in time when their troubles and conflict began. They will nearly always know the time and place where it happened and when things started to go wrong in their lives. If they cannot pinpoint anything definite, prayer is needed that the Lord might reveal the reason either by bringing it to the person's memory or supernaturally. For a person to be free there needs to be a definite act of removal; prayer alone is insufficient. We have to come against all the forces of evil and in the Name of Jesus command that the curse be broken, name the source of the curse and pray that the demonic forces surrounding the curse will be removed. If the source of the curse cannot be found we just have to pray in faith for its removal. We need to pray with the authority of Christ and in His Name.

The removal of a curse does not take hours. But if a person has a curse on them for a long period the effects of it will increase with time, and then the problem can become much more serious. The person can become demonically afflicted, and more concentrated prayer will be needed. In all prayer against the forces of darkness it is wise to pray not alone but in groups of two or more.

A young Western woman who had been working for a period of time in a Far Eastern country came to see me. She had been living with a non-Christian family with other people in the household. On returning home she started to suffer periods of depression and terrible conflict in her mind that was totally alien to her character and nature. Over a period of time and after much thought she came to the conclusion that something had happened to her whilst she had been away. She kept remembering the presence of the cemetery at the back of the house where she had been staying, and wondered if this had anything to do with it. After much discussion and going over every aspect of her visit in detail it became apparent that one factor was beginning to stand out. A member of the household had a terrible and abnormal hatred for her, which had shown itself in various ways when she was staying there. I was absolutely sure that this was the problem as I felt the presence of evil in these incidents. I prayed for the removal of this curse. She returned to normal straight away. Years later I saw her again and the depression and conflict had not returned.

Deliverance from evil spirits

In Mark 1:23-24 the first declaration in the Gospel of Mark of the Sonship of Christ is given by a frightened evil spirit: "Just then a man in their synagogue who was possessed by an evil spirit cried out, 'What do you want with us, Jesus of Nazareth? Have you come to destroy us? I know who you are – the Holy One of God.'"

In Luke 4:35 and Mark 9:20 the demons torment a person severely as the time draws near for Jesus to exorcise the spirits. Luke 4:35 says: "'Be quiet!' Jesus said sternly. 'Come out of him!' Then the demon threw the man down before them all and came out without injuring him."

And in Mark 9:20: "So they brought him. When the spirit saw Jesus, it immediately threw the boy into a convulsion. He fell to the ground and rolled about, foaming at the mouth." Here we see the demons provoked to violent activity before their exposure and expulsion.

In Colossians 2:15 we read: "And having disarmed the powers and authorities, [God] made a public spectacle of them, triumphing over them by the cross." Christ disarms all the evil powers and authorities, and people are delivered by the word of power that He speaks. This is the word that He entrusts to his disciples.

Many Christians, especially in the Western world, have great difficulty in accepting that a Christian can have a demon. However, much of the non-Western world does not have this difficulty; the point is readily accepted and acknowledged. If we have no place for it in our theology then we will be in difficulties trying to help a person in this area.

If a curse is not recognised and remains on a person for a long

> If a curse is not recognised and remains on a person for a long period of time it can have a very serious effect on their spiritual and everyday life.

period of time it can have a very serious effect on their spiritual and everyday life. Deliverance may then be necessary. It could also be necessary in other circumstances, for example, if the person was involved in the occult before they became a Christian, or if a member of their family was involved in occult practices. Sometimes it has come down through the generations. Deliverance involves taking on the powers of darkness or demons that have become deeply embedded in a person's life and praying for their removal in the "Name and power of Jesus Christ". Deliverance is a serious business and should never be done alone, always in a team.

What I have learnt over the years is that in deliverance it is necessary to pray with the authority of Christ, to stand on that authority and not to allow Satan any room for manoeuvre. Satan and demons have to obey the authority of Christ. For example, I would never allow demons to speak or manifest in any way. In deliverance each demon is named and removed from the person's life.

Evil forces can be concentrated in certain locations

In various parts of the world there are areas that as you enter them you can feel the presence of evil. Missionaries speak of areas where they have worked where they could feel the conflict, evil and darkness. It was on one trip to Pakistan that I visited one of these areas. There were holy men and a shrine to which many people flocked if they had a problem or wanted to be healed. There was an atmosphere of evil surrounding me, and I could feel a conflict and something pressing on my mind.

When we had our missions in the Muslim area of East London each person would have to share during the morning prayers and feed-back time what happened in their visitation the previous day. It was not uncommon for someone to say that the home they visited was very dark. So I would ask them, "Was the house the same as the other houses in the street, and were the windows the same size as all the other houses?" They would say, "Yes, all the houses were the same." What they were in fact experiencing were spiritual forces of darkness at work.

Sometimes in the outreach a person would get very depressed; again this was caused by spiritual forces of evil. We would pray with them and the depression would leave. I can remember a person saying once that they felt a stabbing in the back when they visited a certain home. One day on returning from a visit to a mosque the leader of the group found that a blood vessel had broken in his foot and it was swelling rapidly. He went straight to the local hospital, which fortunately was a short distance away. He said that he felt it happen when he was in the mosque. It is easy to put this down to coincidence. But when these incidents happen from time to time you realise that there are spiritual forces of evil very much at work.

A Malaysian girl and her husband were regular members of our church in East London. The wife went home to visit her family on a fairly short visit. Her family were Hindu, and during her visit she slept in the room with the Hindu gods. Shortly after returning home

> In various parts of the world there are areas that as you enter them you can feel the presence of evil.

to Britain she started to suffer depression and to behave in strange ways and appeared to be a totally changed person. The husband became very worried. After a time I began to realise that what had happened to her was not caused by any ordinary means but had some occultic basis. Several of us went and prayed with her. We must never underestimate the demonic forces attached to other religions, and make sure that when we have to draw close to them we pray for the protection of Christ.

I always remember a conversation I had at a conference in South America with one of the speakers, a well-respected Christian leader, who was an expert in the field of Voodoo. I sat opposite him for a meal and tried to learn as much information from him as possible. I can never forget the last words he said to me: "We must never underestimate Satan. More things can be attributed to him than we ever realise. We explain them away, but behind them is the finger of the enemy."

Satan's tactics against Christians

If we are in Christian ministry or witnessing to Muslims we are very vulnerable to attacks by Satan, and we need to know our enemy and his tactics. We are in the front line of attack, and what Satan wants to do is to remove us from our ministry or to stop us evangelising. This is his aim. But how does he do it? There are many ways; let me go over a few:

1. He can cause us to feel lethargic, so that we can hardly keep going. We begin to operate in automatic mode and just force ourselves to continue. Satan makes us feel guilty if we take a break or a holiday. The result is that we reach breaking point.

2. We lose heart or are so discouraged that we want to give up. This can lead to depression. Satan whispers to us that we are not really effective or accomplishing anything and that it is too difficult for Muslims to come to Christ anyway. What the Lord requires of us in this situation is faithfulness. It is He who does the saving; we are only His instruments. We have to stand against discouragement, remembering that we are commanded to do this in the New Testament.

3. Satan attacks the mind. He put dark thoughts into our mind and bombards it. These dark thoughts can increase and increase and lead us down a slippery slope that can lead to conflict and

disunity in our relationships with others. For example we can start thinking bad thoughts or have suspicious thoughts about our colleagues. Often when we analyse what has happened we find that the initial bad thought is a lie and that there is no truth in it. We have believed Satan and a lie. One of the main problems in Christian ministry is interpersonal relationships, and this is one of Satan's main target points. If we look at the Muslim world the history of Christian ministry is one of conflict and division.

4. Lustful thoughts and immorality. One of Satan's targets is to compromise our integrity, and we can fail to recognize this as a Satanic attack. He wants us to be enticed away from holiness and a right relationship with God. We need to guard these jealously.

We need to consider the area of Satanic conflict very carefully in relation to ministry and even in our day to day living. If we are truly effective for Christ the enemy is going to target us and our family. He will try to pick us off, and if he cannot do this he will then target our children. He will also try to destroy us with sickness and death. We need daily to stand against

> If we are truly effective for Christ the enemy is going to target us and our family.

these forces and the evil one, remembering that there is victory in Christ Jesus, the Name that is above every name, to which all will have to bow. When we become Christians we are not setting out on a cruise liner with our sun-hat and sun-tan lotion; we are joining a battleship to fight the enemy and to have victory in Jesus.

BARRIERS HINDERING MUSLIMS FROM COMING TO CHRIST

W hy am I discussing various theological issues in a book about evangelism to Muslims? It is important to realise from the start that in reaching out to people we are trying to search for shared ground without compromising or sacrificing our Gospel. Muslims believe in a God (Allah), the creator of the universe, and this is an important start, but it raises various questions we will have to answer. Also some Christians today say that Muslims worship the same God as Christians do, the Father of our Lord Jesus Christ, and that they have a problem only with the divinity of Jesus. We need to be aware that Muslims too claim that we are worshipping the same God, confirming this by quoting Qur'an 29:46: "Our God and your God is One; and it is to Him we bow."

Central to the Qur'an is an emphasis on absolute monotheism: that God is one and that nothing and no-one can be equal to him. The Arabic word for this is *tawheed*. This is why we need to have a discussion on this topic later in the chapter.

Some Christians argue that the Qur'anic Jesus (called 'Isa) is the same as the biblical Jesus and that the distinctive Muslim view of Jesus is located only in the Islamic traditions or *hadith*. But in fact the Qur'an itself dishonours Jesus, denying that He is the Son of God, the main cornerstone and foundation of our faith. Moreover the Qur'an teaches clearly (Qur'an 9:30) that those who believe that Jesus is the Son of God are infidels and that God curses them: "Christians call Christ the Son of God. That is a saying from their mouth: (In this) they but imitate what the unbelievers of old used to say. Allah's curse be on them: how they are deluded away from the truth."

However the Bible is very clear (John 5:23) that "He who does not honour the Son does not honour the Father, who sent him." In the Bible God is one as Father, Son and Holy Spirit from eternity, a unity but also a Trinity.

A. Are Allah and the Biblical God the same God?

Allah is the unknowable

In Islam Allah is transcendent, or lifted beyond all his creatures, and never has contact with them. He is aloof and distant. Humans cannot even conceive of him or even attempt to know him. He is the unknowable. He does not reveal himself except from behind a barrier or through angels (Qur'an 42:51), although paradoxically he is also said to talk directly and in person with Moses (Qur'an 4:164) and Abraham (Qur'an 37:104-105).

> In Islam Allah is aloof and distant.

Muslims hold that at a later date the Qur'an was given by the angel Gabriel to Muhammad, word perfect from tablets of stone in heaven. They believe that the Torah that was sent to the Jews and the *Injil* that was sent to the Christians were corrupted; God then sent the Qur'an to be the final revelation of God to humankind, and it has now superseded all other books and revelations. Muhammad is also considered to be the final and the greatest of the prophets.

The Biblical God is both immanent and transcendent (or ever present with His people at the same time as being lifted above them). He has made Himself known by speaking to His people in various times and ways and revealing himself to them. The climax of His revelation was when he appeared in the flesh. Hebrews 1:1-2 says: "In the past God spoke to our forefathers through the prophets at many times and in various ways, but in these last days he has spoken to us by his Son, whom he appointed heir of all things, and through whom he made the universe."

The Biblical God is a relational God. From the very beginning, as we see in the book of Genesis, God was walking and talking with Adam in the garden. We read in Genesis 5:24 that even after the fall of humanity Enoch walked with God.

Allah in Islam has different qualities from those of the Biblical God

In the Qur'an there is no mention or discussion of Allah's nature, and that remains hidden and a mystery. In Islam Allah is majestic, almighty and all-powerful and has what they call "ninety-nine beautiful names". The names include the Merciful, the Compassionate, the Wise, the Faithful, the Unchanging, the Creator, the Avenger, Who Causes Death, the First, the Last and the Guide. These 99 names do not denote part of his being but refer to his attributes or to actions by him that he may choose to do, or not. A Muslim can call upon any of these 99 names at any time.

Some of the names and qualities are very different from those of the Biblical God. For example, Allah gives guidance but also leads his people astray[1]. And it says in the Qur'an that when the people were plotting and planning, Allah was the best plotter and planner[2]. In contrast the Biblical God is holy and commands His people to be like Him. 1 Peter 1:15-16 says: "But just as he who called you is holy, so be holy in all you do; for it is written: 'Be holy, because I am holy.'" This same command, "Be holy because I am holy," was given to the Jews in the book of the law three times[3].

A Muslim can only know about Allah – he cannot know him

A Muslim can know Allah only by the names and qualities attributed to him and by his works as described in the Qur'an: creation, judgement and retribution[4]. A Muslim cannot actually know Allah.

In Christianity, in contrast, God is recognised as Father and is involved intimately with His world and people through His Son Jesus. We are able to know God and not only about Him as in Islam. We can have a relationship with Him through the person of the Lord Jesus Christ. God is not someone distant but is ever present with us, totally faithful and trustworthy. A Muslim studying a Bible correspondence course in Pakistan wrote: "I have learned through reading the Bible that God is not a monster to be feared but he has revealed himself as a loving Father through Jesus Christ."

> A Muslim can know Allah only by the names and qualities attributed to him.

Allah in Islam is not a God of love

In Islam Allah remains sovereign, and is omnipotent (all-powerful) and omniscient (knowing all things). He cannot have any human feelings or attributes applied to him, and any idea of friendship or love is considered inappropriate. Here love is seen in terms of an attribute or action of God in response to and as a reward for obedience. Qur'an 3:76 says: "Allah loves those who act aright." And in Qur'an 3:134 we read: "Allah loves those who do good." Sufism tries to overcome this distance by approaching Allah through meditation and *dhikr*, the rhythmic repetitions of certain prayers and phrases until ecstasy is attained.

Conversely Allah does not love the unrighteous and the unbelievers, and Allah does not love those who reject faith[5]. However, the Qur'an does use the word "love" with reference to following Muhammad: "If ye do love Allah, follow me: Allah will love you and forgive you your sins."[6]

The Biblical God loves everyone and is a God of love

In Christianity God is sovereign, holy, just, eternal, omnipotent, omniscient and omnipresent, and as well as loving His creation He is also a God of love. 2 Corinthians 13:11 reads: "And the God of love and peace will be with you."

It was out of love for His creation that God sent His Son. 1 John 4:9 says, "This is how God showed his love among us: He sent his one and only Son into the world that we might live through him."

And John 3:16 is well known: "For God so loved the world that he gave his one and only Son, that whoever believes in him shall not perish but have eternal life."

It is only because God loved us first that we are able to love God. God loves people unconditionally, and His very nature is love.

A Muslim's relationship with Allah

A Muslim's relationship with Allah is one of submission to the will of Allah. The Arabic word *aslama* from which "Islam" was derived means to submit oneself to Allah or to become a Muslim. Muslims often repeat the words *Allahu Akbar*, which mean that Allah is greater than anything or anyone else. The words can be a victory cry to denote the supremacy of Allah and therefore of Islam.

Both good and evil are decreed by Allah

In Islam both good and evil are decreed by Allah. Qur'an 57:22 says: "No misfortune can happen on earth or in your souls but is recorded in a decree before we bring it into existence: That is truly easy for Allah."

And it is Allah who produces faith and unbelief in humans. Qur'an 6:125 says: "Those whom Allah (in his Plan) willeth to guide – he openeth their breast to Islam; Those whom he willeth to leave straying – He maketh their breast close and constricted, as if they had to climb up to the skies: thus doth Allah (heap) the penalty on those who refuse to believe."

> In Islam both good and evil are decreed by Allah.

In Islam there is no concept of free will or free choice

In Islam there is no concept of free will or free choice, as Allah wills what he wills be it either Paradise or damnation or anything else in life. That means that everything is set and cannot be changed. In conversation Muslims often say *Inshallah,* meaning "if Allah wills". This applies to all parts of their lives, which they believe Allah controls. A Muslim will never know whether Allah will grant him or her favour at the last judgement.

Islam denies the crucifixion of Jesus

The Qur'an denies the very heart of Christianity – the crucifixion. In the Qur'an 4:157 we read: "That they said (in boast) 'We killed Christ Jesus the son of Mary, the Messenger of Allah'. But they killed him not nor crucified him. But so it was made to appear to them, and those who differ therein are full of doubts, with no (certain) knowledge but only conjecture to follow. For of a surety they killed him not." This is a clear denial of a historical fact which is at the heart of Christianity.

In John 12:27 Jesus declared clearly in his prayers that he came specifically for the cross: "'Now my heart is troubled, and what shall I say? "Father, save me from this hour"? No, it was for this very reason I came to this hour.'"

Then in Matthew 16:22-23, after Jesus has foretold his crucifixion, we read: "Peter took him aside and began to rebuke him. 'Never, Lord!' he said. 'This shall never happen to you!' Jesus turned and said to Peter, 'Get behind me, Satan! You are a stumbling block to me; you do not have in mind the things of God, but the things of men.'"

Jesus attributed the denying of his death on the cross to Satan and set it over against "the things of God". The crucifixion of Jesus was the eternal plan of God to redeem His creation.

The coming and death of Jesus was predicted in the Old Testament (for example in the Psalms, Isaiah and Zechariah) hundreds of years before the event. Isaiah 53:5 says: "But he was pierced for our transgressions, he was crushed for our iniquities, the punishment that brought us peace was upon him, and by his wounds we are healed."

The crucifixion was an historical fact

According to the Gospels the disciples and the mother of Jesus were at the crucifixion with the Jewish leaders, and they all testified to it. In the book of Acts Peter stands up and challenges the Jews and their leaders, and here again the Holy Spirit confirms that Jesus' death was part of God's eternal plan: "Men of Israel, listen to this: Jesus of Nazareth was a man accredited by God to you by miracles, wonders and signs, which God did among you through him, as you yourselves know. This man was handed over to you by God's set purpose and foreknowledge, and you, with the help of wicked men, put him to death by nailing him to the cross." (Acts 2:22-23)

The historical event of the crucifixion happened in Jerusalem and was according to God's plan and purpose, attested by eyewitnesses and believed in by millions of Christians. Six hundred years later, Muhammad (who came from Arabia, far away from the land of Israel) announced in the Qur'an that the crucifixion happened but that it was not Jesus who died but someone else died in his place. The implications of this are enormous: if true, it would mean that Jesus is not the redeemer and that God's purposes that were set from eternity, foretold by God's prophets and fulfilled in Jesus were false. We need to re-read Matthew 16:23 again.

Allah in Islam and God in the Bible are not the same

We can see from what has been discussed that Allah as described by Islam and the God whom we know as Christians are not the same. For Christians, God is our Father and a God of love in word and action. His nature is love and He is intimately involved with his creation. It is through God first loving us and being the source of love that we are able to love God. That love was expressed to the uttermost by God in the giving of His Son to be crucified. The

We can see that Allah as described by Islam and the God whom we know as Christians are not the same.

love of God is a sacrificial love in that Jesus was willing to be sacrificed for us and we must be willing to sacrifice ourselves for others. There is no concept in the Qur'an of a God of love who can sacrifice or self-sacrifice in thought and action.

B. Muhammad denied the Christian concept of the Trinity

The Trinity appears in the Qur'an and was considered by Muhammad to be the worship of three gods and a form of polytheism[7]. Muhammad thought that Christians believed that God had a physical relationship with Mary that resulted in the birth of Jesus. The first Muslims therefore believed that the Trinity was composed of father, mother and child: God the father, Mary the mother and their son Jesus.

In Qur'an 6:100-101 we read: "And they falsely, having no knowledge, attribute to him sons and daughters ... He is above what they attribute to Him! ... How can He have a son when he hath no consort?" Qur'an 19:35 says, "It is not befitting to (the majesty of) Allah that he should beget a son." Qur'an 19:88-92 expresses great disgust at such a blasphemous idea. And in Qur'an 112 says, "There is Allah, the One and Only; Allah the Eternal ... He hath no son nor father nor partner. There is no person like unto him."

The importance of this *sura* is mentioned in Kenneth Cragg's *The Call of the Minaret*: "It is held to be worth a third of the whole Qur'an and the seven heavens and the seven earths are founded upon it. To confess this verse, a tradition affirms, is to shed one's sins as a man might strip a tree in autumn of its leaves"[8]. This *sura* is recited in daily prayers and indicates how deeply immunised a Muslim's mind is against God incarnate and the Trinity.

Because Muhammad denied the Christian concept of the Trinity, he also taught that it was not possible for God to have a son. However, at the time there were Christian sects who carried the worship of Mary to such a degree that this impression might well have been given to an outsider. In the *Preliminary Discourse* of his 1734 English translation of the Qur'an George Sale mentions a group called the Mariamites who worshipped a Trinity consisting of God, Christ and Mary. The Qur'an also refers to the belief that Mary was considered a third deity and says that both she and her son were venerated as gods[9].

The Trinity sets Christians and Muslims in opposition

In Islam the Trinity is condemned absolutely, as Muslims believe it contradicts the Qur'an and the Islamic concept of God. They consider the Trinity to be blasphemous. The Qur'an even goes as far as to say that Christians who persist in believing in the divine Sonship of Jesus will spend eternity in Hell. It is the Trinity that makes Islam and Christianity diametrically opposed to each other with no hope of reconciliation.

Here we have the absolute monotheism of Islam versus the oneness of the Biblical God. The Qur'an and Islamic teaching emphasise this absolute monotheism, and consequently the first question and argument they raise against Christianity is the issue of our "triune God". We need to affirm to our Muslim friends that Christians believe in only one God. In Mark 12:29, Jesus affirmed the basic Old

> We have the absolute monotheism of Islam versus the oneness of the Biblical God.

Testament confession, "Hear, O Israel, the Lord our God, the Lord is one" (quoting Deuteronomy 6:4-6). James 2:19 says, "You believe that there is one God. Good! Even the demons believe that – and shudder." And in Romans 3:29-30 we read, "Is God the God of the

Jews only? Is he not the God of the Gentiles too? Yes, of Gentiles, too since there is only one God."

The issue of the Trinity is one of the main stumbling blocks that prevent Muslims accepting Christ. In our evangelism to Muslims to attempt to explain the Trinity can often cause great confusion and easily lead to an argument. We need to recognise that this is one of the most difficult topics for Muslims to understand and can raise heated emotions. It is only as we know the Lord Jesus Christ and are indwelt by the Holy Spirit that we are able to understand the depths of this revelation and mystery. However, grappling with the doctrine of the Trinity will ensure that we have the knowledge to answer questions if they should be raised. It is certainly best, if possible, to avoid this subject in the early stages of a relationship with Muslims.

Muhammad spoke out strongly against the Trinity

Muslims believe that to make anything or anyone equal to Allah is the sin of *shirk* or polytheism, which is the most heinous of all sins in Islam. It is considered to be the worst form of idolatry. Muhammad spoke out strongly against the Trinity and considered the Christians to have embraced polytheism.

> **Muhammad spoke out strongly against the Trinity.**

In Qur'an 4:116 we read, "Allah forgiveth not (the sin of) joining other gods with him." The Qur'an states that those that believe in the Trinity are unbelievers, as Jesus was only a prophet or messenger as other messengers before him. Qur'an 5:75 says, "Christ, the son of Mary, was no more than a Messenger; many were the Messengers that passed away before him." And those that teach the Trinity are blasphemers who will be punished severely by being thrown into Hell for eternity. Qur'an 5:73 says, "They do blaspheme who say: Allah is one of three in a Trinity: for there is no god except One God. If they desist not from their word (of blasphemy) verily a grievous penalty will befall the blasphemers among them."

The Holy Spirit in Islam is very ambiguous

The definition of the Holy Spirit in Islam is very ambiguous. When Muhammad was asked about the Spirit, his answer was not clear, as he seems to have been unfamiliar with the true doctrine of the Trinity. In Qur'an 66:12 Jesus is described as the "Spirit of God" breathed into Mary. Qur'an 2:253 says that Jesus was strengthened by the Holy Spirit: "To Jesus the son of Mary we gave clear (signs) and strengthened him with the Holy Spirit." The Qur'an also goes on to say (58:22) that God strengthens all believers with his spirit: "He has written faith in their hearts and strengthened them with a spirit from Himself."

The main point is that like Jesus the Holy Spirit or Spirit of God is not identified as a person of the Trinity in Islam.

The full deity of the Spirit

In Christianity the Holy Spirit has characteristics possessed only by God, and He is recognised as God in Acts 5:3-4: "Then Peter said, 'Ananias, how is it that Satan has so filled your heart that you have lied to the Holy Spirit and have kept for yourself some of the money you have received for the land? ... You have not lied to men but to God."

The Holy Spirit knows the things of God, which implies his omniscience or infinite knowledge, and we are told in Scripture that he is everywhere (or "omnipresent"). He has equality with the Father and Son as an equal.

Matthew 28:19 says, "'Therefore go and make disciples of all nations, baptising them in the name of the Father and of the Son and of the Holy Spirit and teaching them to obey everything I have commanded you.'" And 2 Corinthians 13:14 reads, "May the grace of the Lord Jesus Christ, and the love of God, and the fellowship of the Holy Spirit be with you all."

The work of the Holy Spirit is to sanctify or make holy. 1 Peter 1:2 says, "...who have been chosen according to the foreknowledge of God the Father, through the sanctifying work of the Spirit, for obedience to Jesus Christ and sprinkling by his blood."

He proceeds and is proceeding from the Father and the Son. John 15:26 says, "When the Counsellor comes, whom I will send to you from the Father, the Spirit of truth who goes out from the Father, he will testify about me."

The Christian understanding of the Trinity

The doctrine of the Trinity is a very important doctrine of the Christian faith, although Christians often find the Trinity very difficult to understand. If we examine the history of pre-Islamic Arabia and the early history of Muhammad we will find that the early advisors of Muhammad were Ebionites (members of a heretical sect in the early church). It is easy to see why Muhammad could not comprehend the depth of the Christian doctrine of the Trinity and managed to get it so wrong. Muslim polemics assert that the Trinity is not mentioned as doctrine in the Bible but was invented by the early church councils. They claim that the church distorted Scripture to reach this doctrine.

The word "Trinity" is not mentioned in the Bible, but the concept is. The Trinity is partially revealed in the Old Testament, but the complete revelation comes in the New Testament. It was in 325AD at Nicaea that a Council was convened by the Christian Emperor Constantine and the early doctrine of the Trinity was formulated; it was later established at the Council of Constantinople (381). The delegates agreed that God existed from eternity as the Father, the Son and the Holy Spirit. Out of the Council came the Nicene Creed. We can summarize the Biblical teaching in three statements:

1. God is three persons
2. Each person is fully God
3. There is one God

The Trinity as the full equality of the three persons of the Godhead must be carefully balanced with the unity of God. A more accurate term to use would be "Triune God".

Islam has no concept of Father or family of God

In Islam no human being can be associated with Allah in a family relationship, as Muslims believe this goes against Allah's very nature. Therefore there is no concept of the fatherhood of God, or of a God who can have a close, loving relationship with his people. Allah can have no son, so he cannot be called "father". Muslims see Allah only as creator and judge, not as father, let alone as their father.

> **In Islam there is no concept of the fatherhood of God.**

We are the family of God

In contrast the Bible says that God has bestowed his love on his children by letting them call him "Father". 1 John 3:1 says, "How great is the love the Father has lavished on us, that we should be called children of God!"

We are God's children by the miracle of the new creation through faith in Jesus Christ. John 1:12-13 says, "Yet to all who received him, to those who believed in his name, he gave the right to become children of God – children born not of natural descent, nor of human decision or a husband's will, but born of God."

God is the Father of the Lord Jesus Christ. In Matthew 3:17 we read, "And a voice from heaven said, 'This is my Son, whom I love; with him I am well pleased.'"

In the context of adoption God is "our Father" and we are adopted into the family of God, as Ephesians 2:19 affirms: "Consequently, you are no longer foreigners and aliens, but fellow-citizens with God's people and members of God's household." And Galatians 3:26 speaks of God as the Father of those who believe in Christ.

When one of the disciples asks Jesus to teach them to pray, Jesus says, "When you pray, say 'Father'." (Luke 11:2)

In Christianity Jesus is the mediator between God and humanity

Humanity's need of a mediator is expressed in the book of Job (9:33), where Job longs for an arbitrator between himself and God. In the Old Testament this role was partially fulfilled by Moses as covenant mediator and Aaron and his descendants as high priests. But these were only symbols of Jesus Christ, who is the mediator between God and humans: "For there is one God and one mediator between God and men, the man Christ Jesus" (1 Tim. 2:5). This role is linked to the doctrine of the Trinity and to redemption. In John 14:6 Jesus answered, "'I am the way and the truth and the life. No-one comes to the Father except through me.'" He is fully God and fully human also. Islam has no such mediator between God and humans, though some Muslims believe that Muhammad is a kind of mediator between Allah and humankind at the last judgement.

C. What are the differences between the Biblical Jesus and the Muslim Jesus or *Isa*?

There is a big difference between *Isa* (which is the name given to the Jesus of Islam) and our Jesus, whom we know and read about in the Bible. There are two main sources for the Muslim Jesus: the Qur'an gives a history of his life, while the *hadith* collections establish his place in the Muslim understanding of the end times. However, some Christians who engage in dialogue with Muslims have

> There is a big difference between *Isa* (which is the name given to the Jesus of Islam) and our Jesus, whom we know and read about in the Bible.

argued that the *Isa* found in the Qur'an is essentially the same as the Jesus of the New Testament. If this were true we would have to rewrite and reinterpret all the theology and teachings of our faith.

Isa is only a prophet

Isa (the Muslim Jesus) is a great prophet in Islam, but he is a different person from the Jesus whom we know as the Son of God. To Muslims *Isa* called the son of Mary is merely a messenger or prophet and not the Son of God. The Qur'an says in 5:75, "Christ the son of Mary was no more than a Messenger; many were the messengers that passed away before him." He is, however, considered to be the greatest of the prophets before Muhammad, yet he is human like the prophets of old. *Isa* was a mere man.

Parallels and differences between the Biblical Jesus and the Muslim Isa

THE BIRTH OF *ISA*

The Qur'an states that a "spirit" appeared to Mary and promised her a son. This is assumed by Islamic tradition to have been the angel Gabriel. The messenger goes on to say that the child will be a sign not only for his own people but for all humanity. In Qur'an 19:21 we read, "We wish to appoint him as a sign unto men."

Isa, like Adam, was created from dust and called to life by the will or power of Allah alone. Qur'an 3:59 states, "The similitude of *Isa* before Allah is that of Adam, he created him from dust. Then he said to him 'Be'. And he was."

The Qur'an says that *Isa* was born of Mary, who was a virgin[10]. Mary is mistakenly called Miriam, the sister of Aaron and Moses, whose father was 'Imran[11]. It could be that Muhammad confused Mary with the Old Testament family of Miriam, Aaron and Moses, whose father was 'Amram. There is no mention of Joseph in the Qur'an.

The place where *Isa* was born is not clear, but the Qur'an states that he was born in a remote place under a palm tree[12]. Straight away

Isa comforts Mary in her pain and her fear of people's rejecting her. *Isa* then speaks from the cradle and says (Qur'an 19:30-31), "I am indeed a servant of Allah: he hath given me Revelation and made me a prophet".

There are differences between the virgin births in Christianity and Islam. The virgin birth in Islam was a divine sign but was not indicative of a special role or purpose. *Isa* was created out of the dust of the earth. The Bible says Jesus was born of God (he was not created from the dust of the earth). The virgin birth was the indication of his role as Son of God.

MIRACLES AND *ISA*

The Qur'an says that *Isa* raised the dead and healed the blind and leprous and breathed life into clay birds (Qur'an 3:49). According to this verse (in Arabic) *Isa* did God's work and bore God's attributes (e.g. creator), but he was able to perform miracles only with Allah's permission.

ISA WAS SINLESS

Muslims believe *Isa* was sinless, as in Qur'an 19:19: "(the angel says) I am only a messenger from thy Lord, (To announce) to thee the gift of a holy son."

Isa was the only prophet mentioned in the Qur'an who had these three characteristics mentioned above.

ISA ASCENDED INTO HEAVEN

The Qur'an (4:158) goes on to say that *Isa* ascended into heaven: "Allah raised him up unto himself." One day *Isa* will come again (43:61): "A Sign for the coming of the Hour of Judgement: therefore have no doubt about the Hour but follow ye Me: this is a Straight

> *Isa* is presented as an eschatological figure who has an important role to play in the end times.

Way." In Islam the coming again of *Isa* will be one of the main signs of the last days. He is presented as an eschatological figure who has an important role to play in the end times.

ISA IS CALLED "WORD OF GOD" AND "SPIRIT OF GOD"

Isa is called "Word of God" and "Spirit of God", the only prophet who is called by these names in the Qur'an (4:171): "Christ Jesus the son of Mary was (no more than) a messenger of Allah, and His Word which he bestowed on Mary and a Spirit proceeding from Him." However the Qur'anic *Isa* is only "a" word of God and not "the" Word of God (or the *logos* who was pre-existent with the Father at creation) as described in John 1:1: "In the beginning was the Word, and the Word was with God, and the Word was God."

ISA BROUGHT A GOSPEL TO HUMANKIND

Muslims believe that *Isa* brought a Gospel called the *al-injil* and a law to humankind[13]. This Gospel is nothing like our Gospels or any part of the New Testament and contains *Isa*'s preaching about the unity of Allah and the last judgement. The Qur'an has only one verse relating to the crucifixion, and it denies that *Isa* was crucified. The message *Isa* gives is one confirming the message of earlier prophets. Nothing is mentioned of the life of *Isa* or any content from his teachings. There is also no reference to any content from the book of Acts or any of Paul's epistles.

> **Muslims believe that *Isa* was a mere man, like any other prophet, and that all of them have been superseded by Muhammad.**

ISA WAS HUMAN ONLY

Muslims believe that *Isa* was a mere man, like any other prophet, and that all of them have been superseded by Muhammad. *Isa* was created from dust and lived like other prophets or messengers sent by Allah before him[14].

Christians believe that even though Jesus was fully human, He was also fully God. He had a human body and all the normal human characteristics such as being hungry and thirsty and weary, and that he was perfectly human as well as being fully God, these two natures coming together in one person. As we read in Philippians 2:5-7: "... Christ Jesus ... being in very nature God, did not consider equality with God something to be grasped, but made himself nothing, taking the very nature of a servant, being made in human likeness."

ISA WAS CALLED THE MESSIAH, BUT HE WAS NOT A REDEEMER

Isa is called the Messiah in the Qur'an eleven times. However, the title is another empty one, as it does not carry the Old Testament meaning of "Messiah" or its fulfilment in the Jesus of the New Testament, where it means "Anointed One" and "Redeemer".

ISA WAS NOT THE SON OF GOD

Muslims deny the deity of *Isa* and therefore do not accept him as the Son of God. To them *Isa* is only a messenger. They quote the following *sura* in the Qur'an (4:171): "O People of the Book! Commit no excesses in your religion: nor say of Allah aught but the truth. Christ Jesus the son of Mary was (no more than) a messenger of Allah, and His Word which he bestowed on Mary, and a Spirit proceeding from Him: so believe in Allah and His Messengers. Say not "Trinity" desist. It will be better for you: For Allah is One God: Glory be to Him: (Far Exalted is He) above having a son."

Muslims believe that *Isa* confirms this himself, and says the idea that Allah could have a child is blasphemous. In Qur'an 5:72 we read, "They do blaspheme who say: 'Allah is Christ the son of Mary'. But said Christ 'O Children of Israel! Worship Allah, my Lord and your Lord'. Whoever joins other gods with Allah – Allah will forbid him The Garden, and the Fire will be his abode. There will for the wrong doers be no one to help."

Paramount in Islam is absolute monotheism or the unity of Allah, and this is in direct opposition to the Trinity and therefore the divine nature and Sonship of Jesus Christ. Muhammad believed the idea that Allah should have a son is a lie believed only by those that are ignorant. In the Qur'an 18:4-5 we read: "What they say is nothing but falsehood!"

Islam not only proclaims the unity of God but constantly attacks the Sonship of Christ at every level from its theology to its practice. Muslims consider the statement that "Jesus is the Son of God" to be blasphemous, and it will cause them to react sharply with great disgust[15].

At the right time in evangelism we will need to clarify the true identity of Jesus as the Son of God and point out Islam's incorrect teaching with regard to Mary's having sexual relations with God and producing a child. It needs to be mentioned that this is abhorrent to us as well as them and that Jesus was not the child of God but the Son of God, which is entirely different.

CHRISTIANS BELIEVE THAT JESUS WAS THE SON OF GOD

As Christians we believe that Jesus was the Son of God, and we should not be fearful in proclaiming it to any religion that is out to destroy this crucial point of our faith. Jesus is the very cornerstone and centre of our faith. It is in Him that we put our trust.

JESUS WAS A PERSONAL MANIFESTATION OF THE GODHEAD

His two titles, "Son of God" and the "Word", ensure that we understand Him as a personal manifestation of the Godhead, equal with the Father. He is an accurate expression of God's glory and person. Our Lord is not merely a likeness of the Father but of "one substance with the Father". He and the Father are one. He is described as the Word, the pre-existent Christ, in a unique relationship with the Father.

> As Christians we believe that Jesus was the Son of God.

John 1:14 reads, "The Word became flesh and made his dwelling among us. We have seen his glory, the glory as of the One and Only who came from the Father, full of grace and truth."

Colossians 2:9 states very clearly, "For in Christ all the fullness of the Deity lives in bodily form, and you have been given fullness in Christ, who is the head over every power and authority."

THE ETERNAL NATURE OF THE SON

The word "begotten", not "made", is used of His origin. This means that He was not created, as the angels were. Here we have the eternal nature of the Sonship of Christ. He was the Son of God before time began. In John 1:18 we read: "No one has seen God at any time. The only begotten Son, who is in the bosom of the Father, He has declared Him" (NKJV). John 17:5 says, "And now, Father, glorify me in your presence with the glory I had with you before the world began." And in 1 John 4:9 we read: "This is how God showed his love among us: He sent his one and only Son into the world that we might live through him." In John 1:1, the terms "Logos" or "Word" and "only Son" are applied to the same person.

ISA WAS NOT CRUCIFIED OR RAISED FROM THE DEAD

There is only one verse in the Qur'an about the crucifixion and that verse is very confused as to whether Jesus was crucified or not. Qur'an 4:157-158 says: "That they said (in boast), 'We killed Christ Jesus the son of Mary, the Messenger of Allah' – But they killed him not, nor crucified him, but so it was made to appear to them, and those who differ therein are full of doubts, with no (certain) knowledge, but only conjecture to follow. For of a surety they killed him not – Nay Allah raised him up unto himself; and Allah is exalted in Power, Wise."

> Muslim theology does deny that Jesus was crucified.

However, Muslim theology does deny that Jesus was crucified.

Muhammad would have had no idea of the meaning of the crucifixion: that Jesus died on the cross to provide salvation so that a person's sins might be forgiven, reconciling us to God and giving us the assurance of eternal life.

We need to look at the way Muslims view the crucifixion. They see it as a defeat. If they believed Jesus was crucified it would mean that he established no earthly kingdom and achieved no success; he would have no followers and no legacy. Muslims also see crucifixion, to be nailed on the cross as a criminal, as a disgrace and not worthy of the honour of a prophet.

The most common view in Islam is that the *hadith* (the inspired tradition) and the clerics teach that God substituted someone in Jesus' place who appeared to everyone to be Jesus. Instead of being crucified, they believe, Jesus was eventually taken straight to heaven. It is not clear whom they believe God substituted, but there are many hypotheses, such as Judas, one of the disciples, Simon of Cyrene, a criminal etc. The Ahmadiyya movement (a sect of Islam) believes that Jesus survived the crucifixion, migrated to India and eventually died a natural death.

As they do not believe that Jesus was crucified, they also deny the resurrection.

ISA WILL COME AGAIN

Muslims believe that *Isa* will descend to earth to the *Isa* minaret of the large Umayyad Mosque in Damascus. This was originally the Christian Cathedral in Damascus, which was demolished and rebuilt as a mosque by a Muslim caliph in 709-715. *Isa* will come as a Muslim warrior to destroy Christianity and Judaism and will establish Islam as the only religion in the world. He will fight all its enemies (including the Antichrist *al-Dajjal*).

"Narrated Abu Hurayrah: The Prophet (peace be upon him) said: There is no prophet between me and him, that is *Isa* (peace be upon him). He will descend (to the earth). When you see him, recognise him: a man of medium height, reddish fair, wearing two light yellow garments, looking as if drops were falling down from his head though it will not be wet. He will fight the people for the cause of Islam. He will break the cross, kill swine, and abolish jizyah. Allah will perish all religions except Islam. He will destroy the Antichrist and will live on earth for forty years and then he will die. The Muslims will pray over him." (Sunan Abu Dawood, 4310)

To "break the cross" means to destroy Christianity. Pigs are associated with Christians, as both Muslims and Jews consider them unclean, and the killing of the pigs also refers to the destruction of Christianity. Under Islamic law the humiliating poll-tax (*jizya*) is paid by subjected Christians and Jews to protect them from jihad. The abolition of the poll-tax signifies the revival of jihad against Christians and Jews, who will face the choice of converting to Islam or being killed.

Isa will then marry, have children, die and be buried alongside Muhammad.

JESUS AS THE SON OF GOD THREATENS ISLAMIC THEOLOGY

Jesus as the Son of God challenges the very basis of Allah and Islamic theology. The primary tenet of Muslims' faith, the absolute unity of Allah, is challenged by the deity of Christ. If God has a son, Islam is in error, and that is why this idea has to be so adamantly denied.

> Jesus as the Son of God challenges the very basis of Allah and Islamic theology.

Every Friday at the mosque Qur'an 112 is recited during the service. It says, *"Say, He is Allah the One and Only, Allah the Eternal, Absolute, He begetteth not, nor is He begotten and there is none like unto Him."*

This is a polemic against the Christian confession that Jesus is the only-begotten Son of God. Constantly repeated, it is a denial of Jesus as the Son of God and also of the Trinity. The Muslim call to prayer ("There is no god but Allah and Muhammad is the messenger of God") goes out over the rooftops five times a day from the minaret and is a polemic against both the Sonship and deity of Christ and the Christian faith.

The Muslims have Islamised Jesus into their *Isa* and made him to be the forerunner of but subservient to Muhammad. But Christ cannot forever be robbed of his glory, since the Holy Spirit is the great vindicator of Jesus Christ (John 16:4-15). The Holy Spirit in Muslim polemic is attributed to the coming of Muhammad, yet in the New Testament text it is clear that the Holy Spirit is the third person in the Trinity and the Glorifier of Christ, the Son of the living God.

D. Salvation and Islam

Salvation as we know it in Biblical Christianity does not really exist within Islam; even the word "salvation", has no equivalent in Islamic thought.

Salvation in Christ

In Christianity sin causes separation from a holy God, and our sins are forgiven or blotted out when we receive salvation by the acceptance of Jesus Christ as Lord and Saviour. We look to the cross and resurrection, to Jesus' dying for our sins and rising again for our justification, and to the assurance we have of eternal life. In Christianity there is a definite link between salvation and sin.

In contrast Muslims will understand the phrase "being saved" only in the context of being delivered from hell-fire to Paradise, not in the context of sin's causing separation from God and the assurance of eternal life. Many converts from Islam say that the concept of salvation was the very thing that attracted them to Christ.

In Islam there is no assurance of Paradise

In Islam whether a person will go to Paradise or hell is not clear.

Whilst some texts say that all Muslims will have to go through hell before entering Paradise[16], others indicate that those who believe and do right – the god-fearing – will enter the Gardens of Delight or Paradise[17]. Here we see the linking of believing and doing good works. However, the assurance of one's eternal destiny and escape from the agony of hell-fire is lacking within Islam, and Muslims can only hope for Paradise but with no certainty. We need to share with Muslims that it is possible to have the assurance of heaven through putting our trust in Jesus Christ. This can be a very effective point to share in evangelism as it shows up a severe weakness within Islam.

However, Islam overcomes this weakness by suicide bombings or martyrdom. To fight for Islam or to engage in jihad is considered to be a testimony or *shahada*. The people who take part are called *shahids* (martyrs or witnesses), and their actions are recognised as self-sacrificing and noble. Martyrdom is not considered to be suicide or even related to it. Muslims believe the *shahids* will go immediately to Paradise with all their sins forgiven. This act can be the only assurance of Paradise after death for the Muslim. The martyr can then intercede for seventy of his relatives to enter Paradise immediately on their death[18].

A Muslim woman's destiny in eternity

What happens when a Muslim woman dies? Does she face the same fate as her husband or is there an entirely different set of rules? What happens if a woman decides to become a martyr? One Muslim woman caught before she could blow herself up expected to become "the purest and most beautiful form of angel at the highest level possible in heaven"[19].

However, Muhammad looked into hell and saw that the majority of its inhabitants were women. The *hadith* 301.1 Bukhari says, "Once Allah's Apostle said to a group of women, 'Give alms, as I have seen that the majority of the dwellers of Hell-fire were you (women)'."

This *hadith* and a number of others state that the majority of the people in hell are women. So how does a woman get to Paradise? The answer spelled out elsewhere in the *hadith* is that a woman gets to Paradise by being absolutely obedient to her husband. It is this that shows her piety and guarantees her eternal destiny. He is her Paradise or her hell, and without obedience to her husband there is no heaven for a woman.

The wives of the righteous and obedient are mentioned as accompanying their husbands in Paradise. Women in Paradise must be submissive, subordinate, veiled and secluded in the harems of Paradise, watching quietly as their husbands make love with the beautiful *houris* (perpetual virgins) of Paradise. Man is her master on earth and she will be subjugated to him forever in heaven as well[20]. There is no provision made for single women.

In evangelism to Muslim women sharing about the assurance and hope of Paradise can really speak to their hearts. If they remain within Islam they have a depressing future with no hope before them when they die. We need readily to share how we have this eternal destiny with the Kings of Kings and Lord of Lords and they can have this glorious and eternal future in front of them as well. Many Muslim women come to Christ to find this assurance of salvation.

Judgement day for the Muslim

A Muslim can never be sure of his salvation at the Last Judgement. The first thing to be judged will be prayer. One of the most terrible sins a Muslim can commit is a failure to be at prayer to confess the *shahada*, which renders him an unbeliever and will result in his being thrown into the fires of hell. To avoid hell he must repent before he dies, but even then he can never be sure of his destiny. A Muslim who has fallen into unbelief, like the

> A Muslim can never be sure of his salvation at the Last Judgement.

person who leaves Islam, will suffer the eternal fires of hell. Those who have committed minor sins and have not repented will, after a period in hell, be able to enter Paradise.

At the last judgement all a person's good deeds will be weighed on the scales against the bad deeds. The good deeds are multiplied by ten, and if the good deeds then outweigh the bad deeds the person will be allowed to enter Paradise. A Muslim who has done few good deeds and has not kept the duties and obligations of Islam has little hope of Paradise, and even if he has done numerous good deeds there is always the worry that the bad deeds might outweigh the good deeds. Salvation is by works alone.

Allah decides who will be saved and who will be damned

However in the final analysis "Allah wills what he wills". Qur'an 14:4 reads, "Now Allah leaves straying those whom He pleases and guides whom He pleases." And in Qur'an 7:178 we read: "Whom Allah doth guide – He is on the right path: Whom he rejects from His guidance – such are the persons who perish." It is decided by Allah who will be saved and who will be damned.

> It is decided by Allah who will be saved and who will be damned.

Muslim theologians developed the concept of God's eternal decree. God has determined all things in advance and has written them down in the eternal book of his decrees. These include human actions. Thus my salvation and damnation is decided by God before my birth, and my personal history is merely the working out of God's decree[21]. Muslims hope the final day will reveal that the decree of the Divine has been favourable to them. Consistent with their view, however, they will not be inclined to say "I am saved", but rather to say, "I am saved if God wills"[22].

Sin and Islam

Sin is seen in a completely different way in Islam from how it is seen in Christianity. In Islam there is not the consciousness of sin in relation to a righteous God or of the seriousness of it in relation to faith. Sin is seen more in a legalistic framework as an act of wrongdoing not specifically related to the human heart. Islam distinguishes between the greater and the lesser sins. Greater sins would include adultery, drinking alcohol, murder, homosexuality, false testimony and theft, amongst many others. Greater sins are more serious and will lead to punishment; the lesser sins are common to everyone and can be forgiven or overlooked much more easily. This breaking of the law can be remedied by good deeds.

To a Muslim the most serious sins would be:

1. The sin of *shirk*, associating someone else with Allah. This is an unpardonable sin. And Christians are told that they are guilty of this if they insist that Jesus is the Son of God.
2. The sin of *apostasy* or leaving the Muslim faith, which according to sharia is punishable by death. This can be the barrier to Muslims' coming to Christ and the fear of committing this can bind them to the religion of Islam.
3. Sins such as murder and adultery.

When we talk about Jesus' taking our sin on himself on the cross and giving us forgiveness of sin when we accept him into our life this has little meaning for the Muslim. As Christians we consider ourselves to be sinful in that we constantly do things that are contrary to what God desires.

There is only one true God and all other ways are lost

The Ten Commandments in Exodus: (20:3) make it clear that there is one true God. This is followed through in the New Testament with passages such as 1 Corinthians 8:6: "Yet for us there is but one

God, the Father, from whom all things came and for whom we live; and there is but one Lord, Jesus Christ, through whom all things came and through whom we live. And in Ephesians 4:4-6 we read: "There is one body and one Spirit – just as you were called to one hope when you were called – one Lord, one faith, one baptism; one God and father of all, who is over all and through all and in all."

> It says very clearly in the Bible that there is salvation in no other but Jesus Christ and all other ways are lost.

A good starting point for further conversation is Mark 12:28-29, as Muslims would agree with this: "'Of all the commandments which is the most important?' 'The most important one,' answered Jesus 'is this: "Hear, O Israel, the Lord our God, the Lord is one"'"

However, it is important in our evangelism to Muslims to point out that we believe in one God and not three gods. As well as pointing out that we believe in one God we should mention that God is a triune God: God the Father, God the Son and God the Holy Spirit.

It says very clearly in the Bible that there is salvation in no other but Jesus Christ and all other ways are lost (Acts 4:12; 1 John 5:12). This means that anyone who does not accept Jesus as Lord and Saviour is going to a lost eternity. We have a responsibility as Christians to share the Good News of Jesus Christ with those we come across.

The end times in Islam

Islam has an end-time scenario, which is radically different to that of Christianity. Muslims believe in the lesser and greater signs of the Hour. They believe that humankind will reach a state of great suffering and then the awaited Mahdi will appear. He will be the first of the greater signs of the Hour. The Mahdi will rule until the False Messiah (*al-Masih al Dajjal*) appears, who will spread oppression and corruption. The false Messiah will remain for a while, destroying humankind completely, and the earth will witness the greatest tribulation in its history. Then *Isa* will descend to earth and bring justice. He will kill the false Messiah, and then there will be years of safety and security. Gog and Magog will then appear and surprise humankind, and corruption will take over again. *Isa* prays, and Gog and Magog will die. At a later date *Isa* dies, and he will be buried alongside Muhammad. This is followed by the appearance of the Beast, which leads to the Day of Judgement[23].

And in conclusion

As Christians we see Judaism as a preparation for the coming of Christ. Islam teaches that the Jews corrupted their scriptures, so God sent the *Injil* for the Christians. When they in turn corrupted their scriptures, God then sent the Qur'an as the final revelation of God to humankind, and Muhammad as the final prophet. Muslims say that the Qur'an has superseded the New Testament and see Judaism and Christianity as paving the way for the coming of Islam.

There are no definite dates given to any event in the Qur'an, and there is also a marked absence of place names. Only from the tradition do we know anything about when and where the various chapters were revealed[24]. The Qur'an also makes no reference to current world events outside of Arabia (the location of Muhammad's ministry), with one notable exception. Qur'an 30 mentions the recent defeat of the Byzantines by the Sassanids of Persia[25]. But here the Byzantines are called "The Romans", which is not really correct; the Byzantine armies were predominantly Greek.

In the Old Testament all the countries surrounding Israel are mentioned in various contexts, such as wars, famines, love relationships, kings and prophets and are set within the historical contexts of the day. Paul's missionary journeys in the New Testament can be traced on a map of that time. The geography and chronology of the Old and New Testaments are woven into the entire narrative.

Islam as a religion cannot be critiqued or criticised.

The Christian idea of revelation is that God works in and through history using the prophets and apostles, who are all set in an historical framework. Muslims ignore history. For example the historical Jesus is denied by the Qur'an, in favour of the Qur'an's statements about him. For Islam the Qur'an's statements bear more weight than the facts set in history. All historical evidence is denied.

In Christianity we have the freedom to critique, and over the years our scriptures have been subject to rigorous textual criticism and source analysis. Islam as a religion cannot be critiqued or criticised in this way, as the Qur'an is considered to be the actual words of God. Muslims consider it blasphemy to criticise the words of God. Thus different rules apply to the two religions. Islam needs to be analysed in the light of modern theological scholarship.

Islamic *Da'wa* or Mission

Islam has a *da'wa* or worldwide missionary agenda and is actively seeking converts. In the Western world hundreds of Christians are converting to Islam, principally women, many of whom are unaware of the implications of their actions. Women usually convert to Islam when they marry a Muslim man. What they do not realise is that in Islam there is no casual friendship between the sexes and as a result of even just a casual conversation with a Muslim man a woman can eventually end up marrying him. Many Western women marry Muslim men for what they think is love but find out in a short while that all the man wanted was a visa and an economic future in the West. After the period required by immigration the man often leaves her.

But many Western and Christian men are also converting out

of conviction that Islam is the true path to God. The implications are far-reaching with regard to their faith. How is it they are converting? If a person is a Christian and does not know about their faith they can think that both religions are so close that it does not matter which one they follow. In Islam the religion is all set out very clearly and simply, and is basically a set of rules that covers all situations and circumstances. In comparison Christianity seems to be very complex and a private, individual faith. Islam emphasises the community, and the community spirit that exists in Islam can be very welcoming and appealing.

APPENDIX

Comparing Islam and Christianity

As Islam increasingly confronts us in our modern world it becomes necessary to understand the differences between Islam

Islam

THE QUR'AN

The Qur'an has 114 chapters (*suras*) and is roughly the size of the New Testament. The *suras* are put together in order of length, the longest being at the beginning and the shortest at the end. The exception is the first sura, called "The Opening" or the *al-Fatihah*. Muslims believe that the Qur'an existed eternally in heaven, engraved on a stone tablet in Arabic, and was known as the "Mother of the Book" (Qur'an 13:39, 85:21-22). They believe it was communicated "word perfect" (in Arabic) by the angel Gabriel to Muhammad over a period of 23 years.

Muslims believe that the Bible and all other scriptures have been superseded by the Qur'an. The Qur'an is therefore considered to be the final revelation of Allah to humankind and Muhammad to be the final prophet.

THE PROPHETS

Muslims believe that prophets are people chosen by Allah to remind humankind of himself and to make known his commands. Adam was the first prophet. Some more prominent prophets are Noah the preacher of Allah, Abraham the friend of Allah, Moses the speaker with Allah, John the Baptist and *Isa* (the Muslim Jesus). There are three pre-Islamic prophets, Hud, Salih and Shu'aib, who are not found in any biblical account. There is no difference between the prophets before Muhammad (Qur'an 2:136). Muhammad is considered to be the greatest of the prophets and the seal of the prophets or final prophet. (Qur'an 33:40)

IBRAHIM (ABRAHAM) and his sons *ISMAIL* (Ishmael) AND ISAAC

Hajar (Hagar), *Ibrahim's* (Abraham's) maid, gave birth to *Ismail* (Ishmael). Sarah his wife gave birth to Isaac (Qur'an 14:39). Islamic tradition makes *Ismail* the father of the Arab people, and they believe that it was through this blood-line that Muhammad was born. Tradition also holds that *Ibrahim* and *Ismail* built the cube-shaped *ka'ba* in Mecca. (Quran 2:124-5)

and Christianity. This concise table of the main traditional beliefs in each religion is designed to make our understanding easier. For many people both religions appear similar, but are they really?

Christianity

THE BIBLE

The Bible consists of 66 books written over a period of hundreds of years by over 40 authors in Hebrew, Aramaic and Greek. They wrote under the inspiration of the Holy Spirit:

> ...no prophecy of Scripture came about by the prophet's own interpretation. For prophecy never had its origin in the will of man, but men spoke from God as they were carried along by the Holy Spirit.

2 PETER 1:20-21

THE PROPHETS

The prophets of the Old and New Testament were chosen because of their obedience to God. Jesus was greater than the prophets:

> In the past God spoke to our forefathers through the prophets at many times and in various ways, but in these last days, he has spoken to us by his Son, whom he appointed heir of all things, and through whom he made the universe.

HEBREWS 1:1-2

Jesus had apostles to help Him in His earthly ministry, who then took the Gospel to the world.

ABRAHAM and his sons ISHMAEL and ISAAC

Hagar, Abraham's maid, gave birth to Ishmael (Genesis 16:15) and Sarah, his wife, to Isaac:

> Sarah became pregnant and bore a son to Abraham in his old age, at the very time God had promised him. Abraham gave the name Isaac to the son Sarah bore him.

GENESIS 21:2-3

Islam

ISMAIL THE ONE TO BE SACRIFICED

Muslims believe that Isaac was the son of promise but not the one to be sacrificed. (Qur'an 11:69-73, 37:112-113). *Ismail* was the one to be sacrificed.

Ibrahim's faith was tested by the order to sacrifice his son. Allah sent an angel with a ram, which was sacrificed in the son's place (Qur'an 37:100-111). The Qur'an does not mention the name of this son, but although tradition mentions both sons, from the Middle Ages it was claimed to be *Ismail*. In Islam *Ismail* is regarded as a prophet (Qur'an 2:136). Muslims believe that *Ibrahim* left *Hajar* in Mecca and Allah provided water for them to drink at a place called Zamzam. This place is visited today by Muslims on their pilgrimage to Mecca.

ALLAH (GOD)

God in Islam is called "Allah". The central point of Islam is absolute monotheism, that Allah is one and nothing and no-one can be equal to him. In Arabic this is called *tawheed*.

He is Allah the One and Only.

QUR'AN 112

To make anything or anyone equal to Allah is the sin of *shirk* or polytheism, which is considered the most heinous of all sins. Therefore Islam denies the Trinity and the deity (sonship) of Christ. (Qur'an 4:48)

Muslims are confused about the Christian Trinity, as they believe it consists of God the father, Mary the mother and Jesus their son. (Qur'an 5:116)

ALLAH IS CREATOR OF THE WORLD

Allah is the creator of the world:

That is Allah your Lord! There is no god but He, the Creator of all things.

QUR'AN 6:102

Allah created the heavens and the earth and all between them in six days. (Qur'an 50:38)

Christianity

ISAAC THE ONE TO BE SACRIFICED

Isaac was the chosen son with whom God made his covenant:

> *Then God said "Yes, but your wife Sarah will bear you a son, and you will call*
> *him Isaac. I will establish my covenant with him as an everlasting covenant*
> *for his descendents after him."*

GENESIS 17:19

As a test of his faith God said (to Abraham):

> *"Take your son, your only son, Isaac, whom you love, and go to the region of Moriah.*
> *Sacrifice him there as a burnt offering on one of the mountains I will tell you about."*

GENESIS 22:2

At the last minute the angel of the Lord called from heaven to stop Abraham killing Isaac by presenting him with a ram. Abraham withstood this test of faith. (Genesis 22:9-14)

GOD

God is one in an eternal Trinity consisting of Father, Son and Holy Spirit. The doctrine affirms the full equality of the three persons of the Godhead, which is carefully balanced with the unity of God. The Trinity can be more accurately described as a "Triune God". The three persons are sometimes mentioned together, e.g.:

> *"Therefore go and make disciples of all nations, baptising them in the name of*
> *the Father and of the Son and of the Holy Spirit."*

MATTHEW 28:19

GOD IS THE CREATOR OF THE WORLD

God is the Creator of the world:

> *In the beginning God created the heavens and the earth.*

GENESIS 1:1

Islam

ALLAH CREATED HUMANS FROM EITHER CLAY OR A BLOOD CLOT

Allah created humans from either clay or a blood clot to worship and obey him (Qur'an 32:7, 96:2). He asked his angels for advice in the creation of humans. (Qur'an 2:30)

ADAM CREATED WEAK

Adam was created "weak", i.e. not perfect. (Qur'an 4:28)

THE FALL OF HUMANITY

Here the challenge was between Allah and Satan (Qur'an 7:11-22). Satan was disobedient to Allah because he did not prostrate himself before Adam. Adam and Eve were caught up in this challenge and were tempted by Satan in Paradise.

THE RESULT OF THE FALL

Adam and Eve repented, and Allah accepted their repentance (Qur'an 7:23). Adam and Eve were then cast down to earth without sin (Qur'an 2:36). Their sin was considered to be only a personal lapse and did not bring innate sin on the whole of mankind.

HUMANKIND IS NOT SINFUL

Allah found Muhammad astray (Qur'an.93:7); Muhammad asked for forgiveness (Qur'an 47:19). Allah guided him and granted him forgiveness (Qur'an 48:2). Muslims believe that children are born sinless and man is not innately sinful. People choose whether to sin or not.

ALLAH'S ATTRIBUTES AND ACTIONS

Allah is best understood from his traditional 99 most beautiful names. These names reveal his attributes and include "holy", "eternal", "the hidden", "the light", "the omniscient", "the omnipotent", "the seeing", "the hearing", "the wise", "the dominator", and "the strong and crafty one" (Qur'an 3:54, 8:30). His roles include "the guide", "the provider", "the just", "the gentle", "the harmer", "the withholder", "the avenger", "the abaser" and "the one who leads astray". (Qur'an 6:39)

Christianity

GOD CREATED HUMANS IN HIS OWN IMAGE

So God created man in his own image, in the image of God he created him;
male and female he created them

GENESIS 1:27

ADAM AND EVE CREATED SINLESS

God created Adam and Eve innocent and without sin. (Romans 5:12a)

THE FALL OF HUMANITY

Adam and Eve were tempted in the Garden of Eden on the earth. Satan tempted Eve to sin; Eve then tempted Adam. They both disobeyed God and ate of the forbidden fruit:

When the woman saw the fruit of the tree was good for food ... she took some
and ate it. She also gave some to her husband, who was with her, and he ate it.

GENESIS 3:6

THE RESULT OF THE FALL

Their sin against God resulted in Adam and Eve's being expelled from the Garden of Eden (Genesis 3:23). Their action brought sin and death into the world. (Romans 5:12b)

HUMANKIND IS SINFUL BY NATURE

Humans are innately sinful because they have inherited the nature that came from fallen Adam:

Therefore, just as sin entered the world through one man, and death through sin,
and in this way death came to all men, because all sinned...

ROMANS 5:12

GOD'S ATTRIBUTES AND ACTIONS

God is described in the Bible as eternal, glorious, almighty, merciful, holy, righteous, forgiving, omnipotent, omniscient and incomparable. His actions are loving, just and wise. He is unchanging. He makes, keeps and renews covenant relationships with His people.

Islam

ALLAH IS NOT A GOD OF LOVE

Allah cannot have human feelings or attributes applied to him, and any idea of his love or friendship is inappropriate. He has no love for sinners:

> ...but Allah loveth not those who do wrong.

QUR'AN 3:57

ALLAH IS NOT FATHER

In Islam no human being can be associated with Allah in a family relationship. There is no concept of the fatherhood of Allah or of a God who can have a close relationship with his people.

THE MUSLIM JESUS OR *ISA*

In the Qur'an *Isa* is often called "*Isa* son of Mary". In most places he is called "messenger of Allah" (Qur'an 3:49), but he is also referred to as "servant of Allah" (Qur'an 19:30), the "Masih" (the Messiah, but not in the specific Biblical sense), a "word of Allah" and "a spirit from him".

THE BIRTH OF *ISA*

A "spirit" appeared to Mary and promised a son; tradition says it was the angel Gabriel. *Isa* was born of the Virgin Mary (Qur'an 3:42-47) in a remote place under a palm tree (Qur'an 19:22-23). There is no mention of Joseph in the Qur'an. The infant *Isa* comforts Mary and then speaks from the cradle. There are no angels, no shepherds, no star, no wise men, no Bethlehem, no fleeing to Egypt.

ISA AND THE VIRGIN BIRTH

Isa was born of Mary, who was a virgin, and he is considered only to be human, like the prophets of old. He was created out of dust and called to life by the will or power of Allah alone. (Qur'an 3:59)

Christianity

GOD IS LOVE

God, as well as loving His creation, is a God of love. It was out of love for humankind that He sent His Son:

For God so loved the world that he gave his one and only Son, that whoever believes in him shall not perish but have eternal life

JOHN 3:16

GOD IS FATHER

God has bestowed His love on His people by making them his children:

How great is the love the Father has lavished on us that we should be called children of God!

1 JOHN 3:1

We are adopted into the family of God:

Consequently, you are no longer foreigners and aliens, but fellow-citizens with God's people and members of God's household.

EPHESIANS 2:19

JESUS

The Bible has many names for Jesus. Some are "Creator", "Saviour", "Word", "Holy One", "Image of God", "Lord", "Prince of Peace" and Mediator.

THE BIRTH OF JESUS

Jesus was born of the Virgin Mary and laid in a manger in Bethlehem. A star appeared in the East and later led the wise men to the place where the child was. The shepherds watching over their flocks saw a chorus of angels. Mary and Joseph and the baby Jesus fled to Egypt as Herod sought to kill them. Jesus' birth happened in fulfilment of OT prophecies. (Luke 2:1-20; Matthew 2:1-12)

JESUS WAS BORN OF THE VIRGIN MARY

Jesus was born of the Virgin Mary (Luke 1:34-35) and was both fully human and fully divine:

Islam

ISA WAS HOLY

...to announce to thee the gift of a holy son.

QUR'AN 19:19

ISA IS NOT THE SON OF GOD

Isa was not the Son of God or divine.

> *Christ Jesus the son of Mary was (no more than) a messenger of Allah, and His Word, which he bestowed on Mary, and a Spirit proceeding from Him: so believe in Allah and His Messengers. Say not "Trinity", desist. It will be better for you, for Allah is one God: Glory be to Him (far exalted is He) above having a son.*

QUR'AN 4:171

ISA IS ONLY A PROPHET

Isa is a prophet and messenger of Allah (Qur'an 5:75). He announces Muhammad as the next or last prophet or messenger. (Qur'an 61:6)

ISA PERFORMED MIRACLES

Isa was a miracle worker. With the permission of Allah *Isa* made a clay bird come to life. He healed, raised the dead and knew the unknown. (Qur'an 3:49)

Christianity

The Word became flesh and made his dwelling among us. We have seen his glory, the glory of the One and Only who came from the Father, full of grace and truth.

JOHN 1:14

JESUS WAS SINLESS

Jesus was without sin, but He shared our nature (Hebrews 2:14), and on the cross He became sin so that we might share the righteousness of God:

God made him who had no sin to be sin for us, so that in him we might become the righteousness of God.

2 CORINTHIANS 5:21

JESUS IS THE SON OF GOD

And a voice from heaven said, "This is my Son, whom I love; with him I am well pleased."

MATTHEW 3:17

JESUS IS THE FULFILMENT OF THE PROPHETS

Jesus is the fulfilment of the law and the prophets:

"Do not think I have come to abolish the Law or the Prophets; I have not come to abolish them but to fulfil them."

MATTHEW 5:17

JESUS PERFORMED MIRACLES

Jesus performed miracles during His earthly ministry to reveal His glory:

This, the first of his miraculous signs, Jesus performed at Cana in Galilee. He thus revealed his glory, and his disciples put their faith in him.

JOHN 2:11

These included bringing the dead back to life:

Jesus called in a loud voice, "Lazarus come out!" The dead man came out, his

Islam

ISA DID NOT DIE ON THE CROSS OR RISE FROM THE DEAD

Isa did not die on a cross and he did not rise from the dead. Muslims believe that another man died in his place. They believe that Allah would not allow one of his prophets to die a death of disgrace. (Qur'an 4:157)

ISA ASCENDED TO HEAVEN

Muslims believe that *Isa* ascended to heaven, where he still lives and from where he will one day return. (Qur'an 3:55, 4:157-158)

ISA WILL COME AGAIN BUT AS A MUSLIM

Isa will return to earth as a Muslim at the second coming; he will get married, have children, destroy all crosses and convert all Christians to Islam. Some traditions say he will destroy all Jews. He will kill all swine and rule as a Muslim King, but he will die and be buried alongside Muhammad. (Sahih Muslim vol.1, bk 1, c71, p104)

THE HOLY SPIRIT

The Qur'an speaks very vaguely about a spirit, sometimes called "holy spirit" or *rul al-qudus* (Qur'an 16:102). Muslims identify it as the angel Gabriel.

SIGNS OF THE END TIMES

Muslims believe that only Allah and *Isa* know when the Judgement Day will come. *Isa* has knowledge of the hour. (Qur'an 43:61)

There will be the "lesser signs", which will be an increase of injustice, sin, faithlessness, shamelessness and tribulation. The "greater signs" will be the coming of the *Mahdi,* the rise of the Antichrist (*Dajjal*), the coming of the Beast, and the rising of the sun in the West. The tribulation will be very great; then *Isa* will return bringing

Christianity

hands and feet wrapped with strips of linen and a cloth around his face.

JOHN 11:43-44

JESUS DIED ON THE CROSS AND ROSE AGAIN

Jesus was crucified (Mark 15:25) and died on the cross for the sin of humankind, and He was raised from the dead on the third day.

I passed on to you as of first importance: that Christ died for our sins according to the Scriptures, that he was buried, that he was raised on the third day according to the Scriptures, and that he appeared to Peter, and then to the Twelve.

1 CORINTHIANS 15:3-5

JESUS ASCENDED TO HEAVEN

Jesus ascended to heaven and now sits at the right hand of the Father until the second coming. (Colossians 3:1; 1 Thessalonians 4:16)

JESUS WILL COME AGAIN IN POWER AND GLORY

For the Lord himself will come down from heaven, with a loud command, with the voice of the archangel and with the trumpet call of God, and the dead in Christ will rise first.

1 THESSALONIANS 4:16

THE HOLY SPIRIT

The Holy Spirit is a person of the triune Godhead.

"When the Counsellor comes, whom I will send to you from the Father, the Spirit of truth who goes out from the Father, he will testify about me."

JOHN 15:26

SIGNS OF THE END TIMES

"No-one knows about that day or hour, not even the angels in heaven, nor the Son, but only the Father."

MATTHEW 24:36

Islam

justice from heaven. There follows the appearance of Gog and Magog, when corruption will overtake the earth. *Isa* will pray to Allah, Gog and Magog will die, and stability will return. This will continue until Jesus dies and is buried alongside Muhammad.

JUDGEMENT DAY (*yaum ad-din*)

The angel Israf'il will blow the trumpet (*sur*) to announce the last day. The dead will be resurrected (Qur'an 39:67-75). The balance of good deeds against bad deeds will be weighed on the scales (Qur'an 21:47). Then there will be a sharp bridge (the bridge of *sirat*) like a knife edge for everyone to walk over the hell fire. (Qur'an 23:102-104)

ASSURANCE OF SALVATION

In Islam people may submit to Allah to find forgiveness. There is no certainty of salvation or forgiveness:

...he forgiveth whom He pleaseth and punisheth whom he pleaseth.

QUR'AN 2:284

Only works are taken into account. The *hadiths* serve as a blueprint of how a Muslim should live. The Qur'an and Hadith give five obligatory duties for Muslims to perform: the confession of faith, prayer, fasting, almsgiving and pilgrimage to Mecca.

AFTER DEATH

Muslims believe that at death 'Izra'il, the angel of death, separates the soul from the body (Qur'an 32:11). In the grave there is an examination by the angels Munkar and Nakir of their good and evil deeds as well as their practice of Islam. This can be accompanied by severe torture. Prayer for the dead is considered to be beneficial

Christianity

THE LAST DAY

All must appear before the judgement seat of Christ.

For all must appear before the judgement seat of Christ, that each one may receive
what is due to him for the things done while in the body, whether good or bad.

2 CORINTHIANS 5:10

Those who did not put their faith in Christ will be condemned (John 3:18). For the Christian it is only their works that will be judged.

I tell you the truth, whoever hears my word and believes him who sent me has
eternal life and will not be condemned; he has crossed over from death to life.

JOHN 5:24

ASSURANCE OF SALVATION

Salvation is by faith in the saving work of Jesus on the cross and not by works. God's grace is a free gift; people do not have to work to gain this gift of salvation.

For it is by grace you have been saved, through faith – and this is not from your-
selves, it is the gift of God – not by works, so that no-one can boast.

EPHESIANS 2:8-9

Good works are the fruit of this salvation.

Believing that Jesus died for our sins and rose again brings reconciliation with God, forgiveness of sins and assurance of salvation.

Their sins and lawless acts I [God] will remember no more.

HEBREWS 10:17 (quoting JEREMIAH 31:34)

AFTER DEATH

God alone knows the appointed time when Christ will come again and judge the world. Christ will come again as the "King of Kings" and "Lord of Lords" (Revelation 19:16) in glory (Titus 2:13), accompanied by angels (Matthew 25:31). The dead will be resurrected. (1 Corinthians 15:51-52)

Islam

(59:10). Between death and the Judgement Day (*yaum al-hisab*) the soul rests in the intermediate state of *barzakh*.

PARADISE

Paradise (*janna, firdous*) for the Muslim is a sensuous place of pleasure and joy. The righteous will find beautiful women there with perpetual virginity (*houris*), rich carpets and couches, a plentiful supply of food, fountains of drink and rivers of milk, wine and honey (Qur'an 56:11-38, 88:8-16, 47:15). Paradise is not centred on Allah, and he will not be in fellowship with the righteous.

Martyrs will have all their sins blotted out by Allah and will enter into Paradise immediately on death (Qur'an 3:169). There is no guarantee of direct entry into Paradise for any other Muslim. A woman can get to heaven only by being completely obedient to her husband (Sahih Al Bukhari 2.161). She remains married to him in Paradise.

HELL

Hell (*al-Nar* or *Jahannum*) is a place of fiery torment for sinners (Qur'an 78:21-30). Those in Hell will "neither die nor live" (Qur'an 87:13). There will be boiling water to drink and bitter food to eat that will not satisfy hunger. (Qur'an 88:5-7)

Hell will have seven chambers. The first is purgatorial fire (*Jahannum*) for Muslims. The second is flaming fire (*Laza*) for Christians, which is not eternal. The third is the raging fire (*Hutama*) for Jews, which is not eternal. The fourth is the blazing fire (*Sa'ir*)

Christianity

HEAVEN

Heaven is a perfect place of eternal joy and holiness, where God will be worshipped and served forever. There will be no pain or death.

> *"Now the dwelling of God is with men, and he will live with them. They will be his people, and God himself will be with them and be their God. He will wipe every tear from their eyes. There will be no more death or mourning or crying or pain, for the old order of things has passed away."*

REVELATION 21:3-4

> *No longer will there be any curse. The throne of God and of the Lamb will be in the city, and his servants will serve him.*

REVELATION 22:3

There will also be no marriage in heaven:

> *When the dead rise, they will neither marry or be given in marriage...*

MARK 12:25

Those who have put their faith in Christ will enter heaven and will be rewarded by God for their faithfulness (Revelation 21:7; John 3:36). Through faith in Christ, men and women equally have the certainty of heaven when they die:

> *Jesus said to [Martha], "I am the resurrection and the life. He who believes in me will live, even though he dies; and whoever lives and believes in me will never die. Do you believe this"?*

JOHN 11:25-26

HELL

The Bible presents hell as a place of eternal suffering and punishment.

> *Then they will go away to eternal punishment, but the righteous to eternal life.*

MATTHEW 25:46

Islam

for Sabians, which is not eternal (Qur'an 2:62). The fifth is the scorching fire (*Sakar*) for Zoroastrians. The sixth is the fierce fire (*Jahim*) for idolaters and polytheists, which is eternal. The seventh is the abyss (*Hawiya*) for hypocrites. (Qur'an 101:9)

Muhammad intercedes for Muslims in purgatory (Qur'an 5:69). In the *hadith* it is recorded that Muhammad reported that hell would be full of poor people and women. (Sahih Al Bukhari 2:161)

ANGELS

Muslims believe that angels were created by Allah from fire (Qur'an 7:12). Their role is to praise Allah, protect believers, and to guard the Qur'an. (Qur'an 3:124-125)

There are four important angels: Jibril (Gabriel), Israfil, who blows the trumpet on judgement day, Mika'il (Michael), who brings rain, and Azra'il, the angel of death. There are two angels that record both the good and bad deeds of all humans. (Qur'an 82:10-12)

SATAN

Satan was an angel, but was disobedient to Allah as he would not bow down to Adam and as a result was thrown out of heaven. (Qur'an 2:34)

FAITH IN ISLAM

Faith is the confession with the tongue that "there is no god but Allah, and Muhammad is his messenger", and performing the duties and obligations of the religion.

Christianity

ANGELS

Angels were created by God.

For by him all things were created: things in heaven and on earth, visible and invisible

COLOSSIANS 1:16

Angels surround the throne of God praising and serving Him (Isaiah 6:1-6). Myriads of angels are at God's command. (Matthew 26:53)

Angels are ministering spirits and are sent by God to serve people. They protect, deliver and guide our ways (Hebrews 1:14). The most important angels are Michael the archangel (Jude 1:9) and Gabriel the bearer of good news. (Luke 1:19)

SATAN

He led a heavenly rebellion against God and was cast out of heaven (Revelation 12:7-9). After Judgement Day he will be cast into hell with his fallen angels for eternity:

Then he (Jesus) will say to those on his left, "Depart from me, you who are cursed, into the eternal fire prepared for the devil and his angels."

MATTHEW 25:41

And the devil, who deceived them, was thrown into the lake of burning sulphur, where the beast and the false prophet had been thrown. They will be tormented day and night for ever and ever.

REVELATION 20:10

FAITH IN CHRISTIANITY

Faith is confessing that Jesus Christ is Lord and acknowledging that He died on the cross and rose from the dead (Romans 10:8-9). It is through this that there is forgiveness of sins and eternal life (John 3:36; 5:24). Faith is a personal and living relationship with God through knowing His Son Jesus Christ. (Romans 5:1-2)

NOTES

Preface

1. There are many variations within Islam, as there are within Christianity. In a short book such as this we have to generalise and simplify, so readers should not be surprised if their Muslim friends take a different stance on some issues.

PART I

Chapter 2

1. "UK Muslims Condemn Honor Killings", *BBC News*, 30 September 2003, http://news.bbc.co.uk/1/hi/england/london/3150142.stm (viewed 15 April 2008).

2. Lewis Smith, "A Murderous Clash of Culture", *The Sunday Times*, 5 October 2003, p9.

Chapter 3

1. Justin Rowlatt, "The risks of cousin marriage", *BBC Newsnight*, 16 November 2005.

2. Tania Branigan, "Islamic Weddings leave Women Unprotected", *The Guardian*, 24 November 2003.

3. Mohammad Marmaduke Pickthall, *The Meaning of the Glorious Qur'an*. Translated by Mohammad Marmaduke Pickthall. Birmingham: UK Islamic Mission Dawah Centre, 1997.

Chapter 5

1. Bill Musk, *The Unseen Face of Islam*. London: Monarch Books, 2003, p40.

PART II

Chapter 2

1. William Muir, *Life of Mahomet* vol. 3. Osnabruck: Biblio Verlag, 1988, p61.
2. Qur'an 67:3.
3. Qur'an 40:7.
4. Qur'an 2:102.
5. Qur'an 55:15.
6. Qur'an 51:56.
7. Qur'an 72:1-2.
8. Mustafa Ashour, *The Jinn: In the Qur'an and Sunna*. London: Dar Al-Taqwa, 1989, p16.
9. Qur'an 18:50.
10. Qur'an 7:12.
11. Ashour, *The Jinn*, p16.
12. Ashour, *The Jinn*, p4.
13. Thomas Patrick Hughes, *A Dictionary of Islam*. Lahore: Premier Book House, 1964, pp134-136.
14. Qur'an 72:11.
15. Ashour, *The Jinn*, p8.
16. Richard.C.Foltz, *Animals in Islamic Tradition and Muslim Cultures*. Oxford: Oneworld, 2005, pp130-131.
17. Ashour, *The Jinn*, p22.
18. Ashour, *The Jinn*, pp24-26.
19. Ashour, *The Jinn*, pp17-18.
20. Ashour, *The Jinn*, p19.
21. Ashour, *The Jinn*, p23.
22. Musk, *Unseen Face*, p36.
23. Ashour, *The Jinn*, p55.
24. Ashour, *The Jinn*, p22.
25. Ashour, *The Jinn*, p50.
26. Ashour, *The Jinn*, pp51-63
27. Ashour, *The Jinn*, p13.
28. Musk, *Unseen Face*, p47.
29. Sayyid Qutb, *In the Shade of the Qur'an*. Vol. XVIII. Markfield: The Islamic Foundation, 2004, pp278-281.

Chapter 3

1. Qur'an 14:4, 16:9.
2. Qur'an 8:30.
3. Leviticus 11:44; 19:2; 20:7.
4. Qur'an 32:4.
5. Qur'an 30:45.
6. Qur'an 3:31.
7. Qur'an 4:171-173.
8. Kenneth Cragg, *The Call of the Minaret*. New York: Oxford University Press 1964, p39.
9. C.E. Bosworth, E van Donzel, B.Lewis and Ch.Pellat (eds), *The Encyclopaedia of Islam*. Volume VI. Leiden: E.J.Brill, 1991, p629.
10. Qur'an 19:20-21.
11. Qur'an 19:27-28.
12. Qur'an 19:22-23.
13. Qur'an 5:46.
14. Qur'an 5:75.
15. Qur'an 19:88-92.
16. Qur'an 19:71-72.
17. Qur'an 52:17.
18. Thauria Hamur, interviewed by Joanna Chen, "A Martyr or a Murderer", *Newsweek* 23, February 2004, p68.
19. E.Kohlberg, "Shahid", in Bosworth et al, *Encyclopaedia*. Vol. IX, p204.
20. Rosemary Sookhdeo, *Why Christian Women Convert to Islam*. Virginia: Isaac Publishing, 2007, pp70-71.
21. Roland Miller, *Muslims and the Gospel: Bridging the Gap*. Minnesota: Lutheran University Press, 2004, p72.
22. Miller, Muslims, p74.
23. Ibn Kathir, *The Signs Before the Day of Judgement*. London: Dar al Taqwa Ltd, 1994, p18.
24. Samuel Marinus Zwemer, *The Cross Above the Crescent*. Grand Rapids, MI: Zondervan Publishing House, 1941, p217.
25. H.U.W.Stanton, *The Teaching of the Qur'an*. London: Darf Publishers Ltd, 1987, p24.